HEART & HOME

HEART & HOME

design basics for your soul and living space

Victoria Duerstock

Abingdon Press

HEART & HOME
DESIGN BASICS FOR YOUR SOUL AND LIVING SPACE

Copyright © 2019 by Abingdon Press

Designed by Joy O'Meara

Library of Congress Cataloging-in-Publication Data has been requested.

ISBN 978-1-5018-8103-9

Scripture quotations are taken from the Common English Bible, copyright 2011. Used by permission. All rights reserved.

18 19 20 21 22 23 24 25 26—10 9 8 7 6 5 4 3 2 1

MANUFACTURED IN THE PEOPLE'S REPUBLIC OF CHINA

Heart & Home
Design Basics for Your Soul and Living Space

is dedicated to my readers, young and old alike.
May God bless you and change you as you ponder His word.

Endorsements

Heart & Home is layered with poignant, straight-to-the-heart messages and lovely artistic home decor tips and fun facts. With each page, Victoria Duerstock encourages us to nurture our relationship with God and inspires us to weave that beauty into our decor and style. Let *Heart & Home* be the next beautiful addition to your design and devotional collections.　　— Bethany Jett, home decor novice and award-winning author of *The Cinderella Rule*

As the senior pastor of a church, I think *Heart and Home* is the perfect resource for busy women who love interior design and making their house a home. Victoria Duerstock makes the Bible practical and applicable to every reader and this book is well worth the read.　　— Cyle Young, Sr. Pastor, award winning author and Literary Agent

As soon as I read half of one article on Victoria's website, I immediately texted that web address to my wife. Why? Well, the message of the article spoke specifically to several of the challenges Dawn is facing right now.

There's quite a bit of devotional and teaching material out there for women at the moment. But finding an author that won't simply offer easy answers but cuts through to the heart is rare. I recognized that in Victoria's writing immediately. It's hard to quantify just what those magical ingredients are, but you know them when you see them. And they are fully present and at work with Victoria.

I'm looking forward to talking over her writing with Dawn over the next days. And I have a sneaking suspicion my wife won't be the only family member returning to Victoria's pen for wisdom and spiritual insight!

— Dave Gipson, pastor, composer of Trading Spaces theme

This is an amazing creative concept that both calms the soul and encourages our individual identities in Christ.

— Jane Jenkins Herlong, Best-selling author, Motivational Humorist, and Speaker Hall of Fame

Seldom do I discover a book which ministers to mind, body and soul, but Victoria Duerstock's new *"Heart and Home"* is just such a jewel! I was immediately drawn to the unique design elements through color photographs, and especially the carefully selected accompanying Scripture, meditation and prayer. All of these work together to address one small element of life on which I can meditate all day long (and even bring into my own home through her practical suggestions.) While I am neither an interior designer nor DIY crafter, I *am* someone who embraced "hygge" long before I knew what the word meant – a beauty through coziness and care. You too? Good. My gift list for this special volume is already quite lengthy…

— Lucinda Secrest McDowell, author *Dwelling Places* and *Ordinary Graces*

My friend, Victoria Duerstock, is a walking advertisement for all things lovely, which makes the blessing of holding this decorating book in your hands – a real treat. The essence of who she is, is reflected on each page. You'll be challenged to celebrate all you have, while gathering new ideas to fill your home with the same beauty. Congratulations Victoria! Thank you for making our walls a better place to live!

— LaTan Murphy, Designer LLC/Interior Elegance by Latan, and author of multiple books including *Courageous Women of the Bible, Becoming a Woman of Interior Elegance* and *God's Provision in Tough Times.*

As I read *Heart & Home*, I was captivated not only by the beauty and elegance on every page and in every word, but more importantly I was inspired to see how spaces can transform lives.

Creating a home is a sacred undertaking. Building a home or office that inspires, comforts, engages and transforms hearts leads to healthy individuals, families and communities. I was challenged to think about how our homes can be used to focus us on God; how every color, design and object can strengthen our soul.

I hope that Victoria's book will also inspire you and refresh your heart and home.

— Robert Wallstrom, CEO Vera Bradley

Victoria has brilliantly woven spiritual insights and design tips into a beautiful tapestry of words called 'Heart & Home.' This lovely book will be the perfect gift for my friends who love Jesus and love creating beautiful spaces."

— Michelle Medlock Adams, Award-winning, Bestselling Author of more than 90 books

Father, help me seek you in all areas of my life allowing the Holy Spirit's control, so I will unite with others doing the work you have called us to do by advancing your kingdom.

Unity and Harmony

*Finally, all of you, have **unity** of mind, sympathy,*
brotherly love, a tender heart, and a humble mind.

1 PETER 3:8

A well-coordinated color scheme creates a sense of unity and harmony. Not to be confused with looking matchy-matchy, instead a complementary color scheme unifies an entire home. This unity strengthens the composition of the overall design.

Our family members are not cloned images of one another. We recognize this to be true as we join in marriage and merge two very different lives together into one. Moms witness this because even children from the same family plot their own path. While it would be simpler to think and talk the same, the Holy Spirit allows our thoughts and actions to complement each other while still maintaining our individuality. When we love as Jesus loves, we allow grace to fill the spaces when we disagree. Spirit-filled individuals can turn the world upside down with a unified purpose of bringing glory to God.

design tip

When choosing a color scheme of complementary colors, create a palette that will unify the whole collection of space in your home. Pick three or four colors to use in various shades throughout the house.

the best things in life are eternal

Father, help me learn to take on myself only the tasks you want me to do, so I find balance and please you in all I do and say.

Balance Schmalance

Let all things be done decently and in order.

1 CORINTHIANS 14:40

You won't need to have too many conversations with women today to find that many of us feel overworked, under-rested, and stressed out. Stretched thin by the commitments to our jobs and our families, we take inadequate time to care for ourselves. While the command to do things "decently and in order" might indicate more work to a perfectionist such as myself, it also reveals that there should be balance in our lives to accomplish the purpose God has for us. Achieving balance begins with learning to say "no." Taking on too many burdens breaks us down in the long run.

A room without balance seems awkward and uncomfortable. Research shows that using symmetry for balance makes us happier. Many of us crave a structure that is understandable and definable! As it is in the interior of our home, so it is in our hearts. When we are out of balance in any one area, our happiness takes a nose dive and living a joy-filled, Christ-honoring life will be all but impossible!

design tip

Using symmetry in a room poses the easiest method to achieve balance.
Work with symmetry by using a pair of matching nightstands, table lamps, or even artwork.

*I thank you, Lord, that you are acquainted
with our humanity and understand
our deepest longings and needs.
I praise you for your mercy and comfort
you provide your children!*

Bringing Hygge Home

Blessed be the God and Father of our Lord Jesus Christ, the Father of mercies and God of all comfort, who comforts us in all our affliction.

II CORINTHIANS 1:3

What in the world is Hygge? Pronounced "hue-guh," the Danish word references feeling cozy and special. Bringing this sense of happiness to our homes and comfortable living is Hygge. Wouldn't you agree that this should be a goal for our homes? A place of rest, comfort, warmth and calm—a haven amid life's storms. Hygge makes our family and friends feel comfortable and special.

In the reality of the harsh world in which we live, how often do we struggle to find a place of hygge in our hearts? This passage reminds me that our source of true rest and comfort is found in God alone! Even His name reveals hygge: "the Father of Mercies and the God of all Comfort!" He provides our place of rest. No matter the trial or test, He provides all the comfort we need.

design tip

You can achieve hygge with a few simple steps—even a well-placed blanket or fuzzy pillow will do the trick! A cozy home involves thoughtful touches. Thinking ahead about what others enjoy will help us provide for their comfort and rest.

Lord, please help me keep short accounts with you by confessing
my sin daily, instead of accumulating the clutter that will hinder me
from running my race and pleasing You.

No Room in the Room

Let us also lay aside every encumbrance, and the sin which so easily entangles us,
and let us run with endurance the race that is set before us.

HEBREWS 12:1B

Excess stuff weighs us down with the burden of finding places to keep and organize it all. From pillows to lamps, to collectibles and dishes, stuff crowds our homes and our lives. Best course of action: eliminate the clutter. Even organized clutter is still clutter. Whether it exists out in the open or in the secret places we hide it, it is still excess.

Isn't that just like sin? We all deal with sin. All of us. Whether it is a recurring sin we struggle to get the victory over or new roots of sin in our hearts, no one is exempt. Ridding our homes of clutter and creating a simple style helps us enjoy our space more. The same holds true in our hearts. Following Christ is only possible when we purge sin and pursue holiness. The calm a purge offers far outweighs the pain. What are we waiting for?

design tip

Clutter builds up for everyone. Don't organize it! Utilize a system of removing one thing for each new item purchased. Save only the things that bring you the MOST joy. Take pictures of the rest and pass it on.

Dear Lord, I pray that you will continue to expose my sinful thoughts to the truth of your Word, so I will learn to take every thought captive and not wander.

I'm Feeling Exposed

We are taking every thought captive to the obedience of Christ.

II Corinthians 10:5b

The stunning brick work in a local restored industrial cotton mill turned apartment building makes an amazing backdrop for displaying furniture and accessories. A current trend, the use of exposed brick walls in our homes hasn't always been en vogue. Many homeowners have covered up and painted over these brick walls for years!

I'm reminded of my own tendency to cover up my sin. Using a strong word picture from the previous verse, Paul reminds us this is a spiritual battle. The devil desires a stronghold in our hearts. This is only possible when we allow our minds to drift away from truth. Confessing our sinful tendencies, we should instead seek His face when we are fearful, defeated, and desperate.

Exposing our thoughts to the truth of God's word should be a routine habit. This enables us to take our thoughts captive thereby yielding to the Holy Spirit's power to handle our jobs, assignments, and families with grace and compassion. Let's not miss out!

design tip

Exposed brick walls are an exciting interior feature in homes. They add texture and warmth that a flat wall can't give and are used in a variety of decorating styles including industrial and rustic.

Please Lord, take all my fears. You alone are powerful enough to fix it all. I praise you for your peace and protection.

Peace and Calm

Be anxious for nothing...present your requests to God. And the peace of God...
will guard your hearts and your minds in Christ Jesus.

PHILIPPIANS 4:6-7

I have found through the years that we struggle with our thoughts. We battle insecurities, anxiety, doubt, and despair and that's just our mornings! I am not making light of these very real emotions, instead I want you to know that it doesn't have to be this way.

Just as you may not wish to have puke green shag carpet, or dark wood planking in your home, neither should you fill your heart and mind with negative thoughts and debilitating worry. Instead, leave these all at the feet of the One who controls the universe. Acknowledging our vulnerability, we can reach out and ask Him to guard our heart and mind.

Filling our homes with only the things we love reminds us to remove all our worries. Remove that green shag and wood paneling once and for all and rest in the peace God brings.

— *design tip* —

It's best to remove or change the things we dislike in a home. Sometimes that means we must save up to afford a project like that, but it is always worth it in the end because of the peace and calm it brings.

Father, return us to your Word and your "rules" to instill in ourselves the balance we seek. Thank you for providing your Word to us so that we might always have access to the truth.

What? There's a Rule Book?

And he said to him, "You shall love the Lord your God with all your heart and with all your soul and with all your mind. This is the great and first commandment. And a second is like it: You shall love your neighbor as yourself."

MATTHEW 22:37-39

Knowing the rules of good design sets the stage for employing good fundamentals. Sometimes these rules apply to the measurement of a room while hanging curtains or arranging furniture. There are even certain rules that apply to rug placement in a room. Applying the rules ensures the process of good design and creates a well-balanced room.

It's not enough to know the rules in our spiritual lives either. The application of the fundamentals means taking it to the next level. Unfortunately, while applying Scriptural truths and principles to our lives, we may end up adding too many "to-do's." Only by returning to the basics—the foundational rules—can we restore our souls to the peace and sanity that God's Word will bring to our hearts. Knowing the rules brings balance to our harried and hurried souls.

design tip

A good rule to follow for placing a coffee table in front of the sofa is to maintain 15–18 inches of space for ease of movement!

You are my HOME and my ADVENTURE all at once

Lord, I pray that you'll empty me of myself and fill me up with more of You. May I think your thoughts, your desires and your ways, and show the world the difference you are making in me.

Blank Space

Finally, brethren, whatsoever things are true, whatsoever things are honest, whatsoever things are just, whatsoever things are pure, whatsoever things are lovely, whatsoever things are of good report...think on these things.

PHILIPPIANS 4:8

A popular topic in blogs and books over the last decade, clutter occurs at all stages and phases. Whether we are discussing clutter in our homes or minds, none of us are immune. Homes become cluttered quickly if we don't have a system in place to eliminate the excess on a regular basis. It takes just one episode of *Hoarders* to get me rushing around the house trying to declutter!

In our home interiors, the concept of negative space creates the feeling of calm. A cluttered room envelops us in chaos. A cluttered mind because of the desires of the flesh, the lust of the eyes and the pride of life, overwhelms us with anxiety. Paul reminds us in this passage that we are to think on the things that are pure and lovely knowing that God's peace will keep our hearts and minds. (v.7)

design tip

Less is more especially in home decorating. If you find you have too much stuff but don't want to purge, set some pieces aside—accessories, art, or even furniture—and rotate them in at different times.

Father, remind me of my need for You daily. Let me never forget that peace will flow in my life as I continue to grow and consistently walk in grace with You.

Go with the Flow

You keep him in perfect peace whose mind is stayed on you, because he trusts in you.

ISAIAH 26:3

The concept of flow appears not only in interior design, but also in music, nature, and even the human body. A heart blockage forces too much pressure causing a heart attack. A river flows freely where it needs to go without obstacles in its way. Musical flow creates an experience that is seamless. Our homes need pathways that flow throughout our rooms and down hallways. Spacing is important in each room so that no one is tripping over obstacles.

Our Christian walk must also remain clear of obstacles that prevent the peace of God to rule our hearts and minds. Obstacles are burdens we aren't meant to carry. Carrying the weight of financial pressure, illness, and job loss will prevent that peace. Burdens are better left at Jesus' feet because we demonstrate our trust as we do. Keeping short accounts and walking in relationship requires a consistent daily walk. When my mind is tuned to God's Word and His ways, His peace has the freedom to rule my heart.

design tip

Keep hallways and room walkways clear of obstacles. In the bedroom allow 30–36 inches for a pathway as easy access to the bathroom or middle of the night kitchen runs!

*Gracious sweet Savior of my soul, forgive me for straying off point
and turn my gaze once again towards your lovely face.
Remind me to return with my focus fixed on you!*

All Eyes on Him

Let your eyes look directly forward, and your gaze be straight before you.

PROVERBS 4:25

Position and size determine the focal point of a room. In a home with rich architectural details this might be a fireplace, a built-in set of bookcases, or a special window or group of windows like a picture window. Without those details a focal point for the room can still be created with the sizing and use of furniture, art, or dramatic wall color. Characterized by being the first thing you see when you enter a room, the focal point draws your eye forward, directly to the object.

As I write these words, I wonder what the focal point might be of your heart. I know how simple it is for my heart to be drawn from the important things that Christ has for me and to become caught up in the meaningless chaff of daily living. Maybe you have lost sight yourself and need to be reminded that the focal point of a heart reclaimed and renewed by God's grace is indeed our Creator himself.

―― *design tip* ――

If your room has a
built in focal point, fantastic!
Keep it simple! If not,
a large sofa
or beautiful wall art
can become that
feature without
any difficulty.

I thank you, Lord, so much for the gift of the light of Your Word that you have given to us! Empower me to share this Light with a world in need.

Sitting in the Dark

Thy word is a lamp unto my feet, and a light unto my path.

PSALM 119:105

Making a house a home requires certain finishing touches. Many times, we focus on the big details, and then have no energy or funds for finishing off the rooms we are decorating. This is unfortunate because these details are often necessary not just aesthetic. Recently a pair of newlyweds in our small group realized that their apartment living room had no light source at all. They quickly realized they needed lamps, or they would be sitting in the dark each evening!

God's Word as a lamp and a light shines in the dark corners of our hearts and minds and reveals what we could not otherwise see. Without the light of His Word to illuminate our hearts, we will remain unchanged and sinful. Just as we need this light to shine in our hearts, we should also in turn work to shine light into the darkness of this world.

design tip

In the final stages of finishing a room, be sure to save some funds for a pair of table lamps and even a statement floor lamp. These pieces add so much to your room with specific lighting spots and can add an interesting texture even when they aren't in use.

Lord, I thank you for the reminder today that we are a royal priesthood, daughters of the King. We are just passing through awaiting our future heavenly home one day soon!

Blessed with Royalty

But ye are a chosen generation, a royal priesthood, an holy nation, a peculiar people…

1 Peter 2:9

*E*ach year the fashion and design industry name new trends for the coming year. These trends cover not only finishes and fine touches but also color. Pantone releases a "Color of the Year" and designers work to incorporate this color into art, fashion, and homes. Recently, the color named was Ultraviolet—a dramatic purple shade.

Prompted by the new color choice, I thought of adding some ultraviolet, or purple hues around our home. The Bible speaks of purple and we know it represents royalty. As children of God, we are considered part of that royal lineage. Think of it, a specially placed blanket or pillow in our home can remind us of who we are in Christ. Couldn't we all use a reminder that this world is not our home on those long days—the days that are falling apart, when we are desperate and in pain? Our final destination is in heavenly places with our Father the King of Kings and Lord of Lords!

design tip

Yearly trends come and go. Don't invest a lot of money, instead find inexpensive ways to add accessories, pillows, or wall art to highlight a special color.

*Lord, I pray that I will pursue you by being intentional
with my time and energy as I meditate on your Word.
Do the transformational work in my heart and
mind so that I may look like you.*

Look in the Mirror

This Book of the Law shall not depart from your mouth, but you shall meditate on it day and night.

JOSHUA 1:8

Understanding the importance of balance in home design means considering how symmetry can assist us. Symmetry provides balance by using mirror images on two different sides of a central axis point. While these images don't have to be exact matches, the closer in similarity they are, the easier the symmetry is to feel.

Becoming like Christ should be the goal of Christ followers, but this doesn't occur automatically. While we are filled with the Holy Spirit at salvation, we must also choose to work through that Holy Spirit power to do in us the sanctifying work of becoming like Christ. Scripture teaches us to conform our minds and patterns through the Holy Spirit's help, but this passage specifies our responsibility in this process. Meditating on God's Word requires time and patience. In today's climate this is practically impossible without intentional discipline. But skipping this step stunts our growth.

design tip

Using symmetry in a room requires an understanding of your central axis point and placing two pieces on either side. A pair of lamps, wall art pieces, or topiaries can help with creating symmetry.

Lord, help me remember to not always be busy doing, but rather to be flexible with my time to include those you love by inviting them into my space in comfort and rest.

Swing the Doors Open

But only one thing is necessary. Mary has chosen the good portion.

LUKE 10:42

Mary knew that her best task was found at Jesus' feet. I think maybe Mary chose wisely because she knew that her time with Jesus was short. She had learned from Him and sat at his feet. She knew He would not always be with her.

As life flies by, recognize that our family and friends won't always be with us. Making our homes a safe place to land must be important. This doesn't mean that we must have the nicest furniture, the latest trends, or the finest décor. No, rather, it's the attitude with which we open our homes and invite others in to sit, to communicate, to love. May we always be mindful to value others. Fluff the pillows, pour the coffee, and invite your friends over. Invite the neighbors and the strangers too while you are at it and get to know those around you.

design tip

Swinging open the door requires some planning. Keep certain main areas of your home cleaned up each day so that if someone drops in you don't feel horrible about the mess. Keep a stash of ready-to-make lemonade, coffee, and some special cookies for a quick nibble in case of a guest.

Father, as we walk in faith believing what we cannot see, I pray that you'll guide each step and help us to be bold as we declare truth!

Believing Is Seeing

Now faith is the assurance of what we hope for and the certainty of what we do not see.

HEBREWS 11:1

Imagining an empty room with the right paint, curtains, furniture, and art work can be difficult. Others look at a blank canvas and see all the possibilities without effort. No matter which you are, the truth is that you still must take it on faith that each of the decisions you make to fill that room will all work together. No one enjoys making a terrible paint decision, or even worse choosing furniture that doesn't even fit in a room!

Living by faith isn't optional as a Christian—it's essential. Without faith it's impossible to please God. Why? Because we declare to be true that which we haven't seen. Today's society desires to see it first to believe it. We must run counterintuitively in the opposite direction choosing to believe that God's Word is true and holy. We believe what we cannot see because we have applied the truth of His word to our lives and we have found Him faithful.

design tip

Before you order the paint, or even think about furniture, be sure you have a clear understanding of the room's function. The activities planned for this space will affect the decisions from there—so settle it first to avoid mistakes!

Thank you, Lord, for the beauty of the body of Christ. Help me remember our differences, help us to fulfill our purpose in our own special way.

Variety of Styles—One Body

For by one Spirit we were all baptized into one body, whether Jews or Greeks,
whether slaves or free, and we were all made to drink of one Spirit.

I Corinthians 12:13

Frequently changing styles makes it challenging to stay on the front end of every new trend. Depending on who you talk to, more than fifteen different style categories exist in design with many subcategories under them. Many of our favorite designers and professionals are known for a certain style. We each gravitate to certain styles naturally.

Isn't that just like the body of Christ? We all have different tastes, likes and dislikes, and God uses all in different ways. We are each equipped with what we need for the purpose he has called us to accomplish. Our uniqueness and individuality allow us to be used by Him in different ways to reach different people with our unique giftedness while maintaining singleness of purpose—bringing glory to God.

— *design tip* —

Décor and design shouldn't be stagnant or impersonal. Rather, it should flow with personality, evolve with your tastes, and be a representation of pieces that make your heart sing. Fill a house with décor and it remains just a house. Fill a house with pieces tied to memories and it becomes a home.

—Sarah Symonds, www.graceinmyspace.com, Insta: @graceinmyspace

Help me to see the
world as you see it,
Lord, and cause me
to act with justice
and mercy in light
of that view.

The Midas Touch?

What does the Lord require of you? To act justly and to love mercy and to walk humbly with your God.

MICAH 6:8

*I*n design as in life, we must keep the main thing, the main thing. We all struggle to keep our priorities front and center. Staying on task requires living intentionally.

Look around. The world frays at breakneck speed and what people need more than anything is Jesus. We possess the good news to share—The Hope for a world in need—and must share it. We demonstrate His love by following our verse:

- *Act justly—fairness, sincerity, honesty, and integrity*
- *Love mercy—gentleness, kindness, grace, and forgiveness*
- *Walk humbly with your God—humble, peaceful, and always pointing to the One who is the reason for it all.*

Keeping the main thing in design means not being distracted by every shiny little object. Just as we get too busy in life with too many things, even good things, we can create busy designs that take away from our original design.

design tip

Too much of a good thing is still too much. If you love shiny metallics, using them sparingly keeps them interesting and catches the eye, but if like King Midas you want to cover everything in gold, well... you remember how that story turned out!

When my failure and sin loom large, Lord, I thank you, your Word reminds me I am made in your image and design.

Created by Design

I praise you because I am fearfully and wonderfully made.

PSALM 139:14A

Creators relish constructing something from nothing. As the Creator of all things, I see His design and order in everything around me. From the intricate web design the spider weaves, and the way new synapses generate in our brain with new tasks, the touch of the Creator is evident everywhere. Many times, we think of furniture and accessories being created in a factory as untouched by human hands. But today, all around the world, woven chairs, accent pieces, tables, and even lamps are created in factories by hand and only a small number can be created each day.

At times we fail to recognize the Creator's hand in our own lives. Psalms reminds me that before we were even born, we had been created by the Master Designer. We know that his works like the sun, moon, and stars are wonderful; why then do we believe that we are any less? If you are in the midst of a battle or discouragement, I pray you'll look to the one who created and designed you to be uniquely you.

design tip

In many countries today, furniture making still occurs by human hand. The process touched by skilled craftsmen who work many hours refining their creations. Celebrate craftsmanship around the world by selecting beautiful things from many locations.

*Father,
today I thank you for
your patience with
me as I take
the wrong turn
and fail to trust you.
Help me remember
to lean on you for
direction and to know
that the path lies
straight ahead.*

Going in Circles

Trust in the Lord with all your heart and lean not unto thine own understanding.
In all thy ways acknowledge Him and He will make your paths straight.

PROVERBS 3:5-6

Decorating with patterns creates texture. Geometric shapes are especially appealing to those who love the traditional sense of balance that a symmetrical design offers. Hexagons, squares, and circles all create interesting dimension in an otherwise flat surface.

While circles are fantastic in our décor, they are not desirable when it comes to choosing a path to walk. I've seen a few circular paths in my life. I don't always learn a lesson thoroughly, like patience or faith, and I find myself walking down a difficult road once again to hopefully learn better next time. Yet, I'm promised a straight path by relying on God. I'm not sure why we don't follow faster, but when the promise is given, we should learn to trust and obey.

design tip

Using the same geometric feature in a room can be incredibly effective. Having circles in the art on your wall, circular vases on a nightstand or table, and circles or even half circles in throw pillows or a blanket can all tie together creating a beautiful design element.

Lord, I pray you'll keep my heart clean, wholeheartedly in tune with you so I may draw others to you by the words of my mouth.

Come on In

Let no corrupting talk come out of your mouths, but only such as is good for building up.

<small>EPHESIANS 4:29</small>

*T*he entrance of our homes either welcomes friends and family or not. Front entrance or side door, your entrance needs to be easily accessible and inviting. A cluttered entrance is uncomfortable for those entering and they will feel as if they are intruding. This means you need a "less is more" philosophy.

As I think about my heart and the overflow of it, my mouth can be the quickest means of method to overflow from the heart. When the attitudes of my heart are not in line with the Lord, then I can be sure that my mouth is not building up others, not giving grace, and is grieving the Holy Spirit. My mouth as the doorway to my heart indicates the state of my heart. When my heart is off track, I will find it difficult to be kind and gentle. There's no easier way to drive those we love and care about far away from us.

design tip

Consider using lighter colors for your entrance area and keep the clutter hidden in baskets, or a skinny cabinet with doors or drawers. Keep an eye on the things that get laid down or left close by and keep it picked up regularly.

*Father, thank you for
your patience to teach
me to pray, help me
to be faithful.*

Learning by Imitation

One of His disciples said to Him, "Lord, teach us to pray just as John also taught his disciples."

LUKE 11:1B

Pinterest and Instagram have made it simpler to copy style. Imitation is the sincerest form of flattery, so they say. If you find someone who does things well, copying what they do for a time until you build knowledge and confidence makes perfect sense. You are learning about the process and saving a ton of time.

The disciples showed similar insight by asking the Lord to teach them to pray. He was the perfect example and the perfect teacher, and He was with them—walking and talking with them and living alongside them. What better opportunity to learn from the Master himself! I believe that's why the Lord went ahead and taught them. They were willing to learn something they readily admitted was lacking in them, knowing it was necessary for them to be good disciples of Christ. Today we have the written account of His words, we need only to read them and apply.

design tip

Don't be afraid to copy others' style. If you see a room you love, use that picture to find the pieces to put the same room together for yourself. An inspiration picture can help you identify the things you really do want.

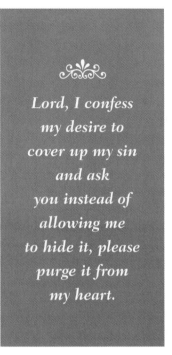

Lord, I confess
my desire to
cover up my sin
and ask
you instead of
allowing me
to hide it, please
purge it from
my heart.

Something to Hide

You are like whitewashed tombs, which on the outside appear beautiful,
but inside they are full of dead men's bones and all uncleanness.

MATTHEW 23:27

When the kids were small, we lived in a lovely neighborhood with a HOA and a set of covenants. These standards applied to the exterior maintenance of our homes: the yard, paint, and basic care including where to place a basketball hoop. Open the front doors of our home during those years and at any given moment there could be laundry on the sofa, spilled juice, cheerios, and toys in the kitchen, and chaos at full tilt. I'm thankful no set of standards existed for our interiors during those years!

Can you relate? As we clean up, fluff the pillows, and hide the clutter out of sight, are we missing the fact that a complete overhaul might be necessary? Do we put on a mask in public, asking everyone to be on their best behavior, but attitudes and tempers are raging just below the surface? We work so hard to show we have it all together, but we hide the dirt inside thinking no one can see it, just like the tombs of old that were full of dead men's bones.

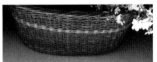

design tip

Keep baskets and boxes with lids handy for those quick cleanup efforts. Last minute straightening can be handled with strategic storage placement.

Lord, I praise you for being the true source of my strength in this life. Help me stay connected and not be too busy for you.

Where's My Power Cord?

I am the vine, you are the branches; he who abides in Me and I in him, he bears much fruit.

JOHN 15:5

I rarely return from a home store or plant nursery without plants, or a fresh floral bouquet from the grocery store or farmers market. Beautiful florals are temporary though because the moment the flower is cut from its stem the countdown begins. No matter how much water or nutrients you provide, the life expectancy is short.

John reminds us that the True Vine is Jesus, and if we will bear much fruit in this life, we must remain connected to him. The moment we break off and forget that He is our source of power and strength is when we start to decline. We can pretend for a little while to still have it together, but eventually we wilt and, in the end, become a stinky decaying mess.

design tip

I love to decorate with natural elements like plants, woods and metals, and neutral fabrics and colors. When I want to change things up (which I like to do OFTEN!), I like to add color in small doses often using seasonal flowers and décor items like pillows that are easy to swap in and out. This way my décor is in harmony with the seasons and constantly feeling fresh without stressing my budget.

—Jodie Kammerer, www.TheDesignTwins.com, IG @jodie.thedesigntwins

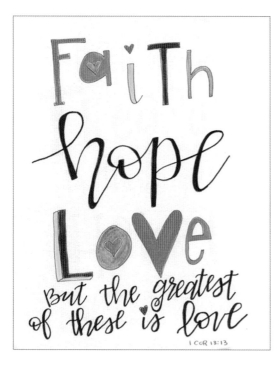

Father, help me to remember that the number one thing
I can do for my household is to demonstrate your love.

The Gong Show

If I speak in the tongues of men and of angels, but have not love, I am a noisy gong or a clanging cymbal.

I Corinthians 13:1

A variety of things fills our homes. We have both necessities like beds, lamps, and refrigerators, and niceties like televisions, microwaves, and air fryers. We even have things that may have had a lovely form, but their function isn't what was advertised or expected. They were beautiful to look at, had a streamlined design, or an awesome concept, but their function doesn't work as promised, or we don't use it as often as we thought we would.

Paul reminds us in this chapter that our hearts can be filled with all manner of things besides essentials as well. No matter how many talents or gifts you may have been given, if we do anything while lacking love, we are just like those clunky gadgets. Great in theory but sitting on a shelf collecting dust. Faith, hope, and love are foundational elements that we must be willing to cultivate and elevate in our homes with Love being the greatest gift we give our families and friends.

design tip

After deciding the function of a room, create your plan for the furniture in that room. Keeping your priorities straight will keep you from filling a space full of unimportant items just because they shine.

Thank you, Lord, for the truth of your Word that teaches
me to continue to confess my sin and forsake it so that
I may walk in the Light.

Keep the Nightlight On

But if we walk in the light, as he is in the light, we have fellowship one with another,
and the blood of Jesus Christ his Son cleanseth us from all sin.

I John 1:7-9

Have you considered the necessity of nightlights? Many have experienced a fear of the dark. Leaving a light on helps alleviate that fear. Guests also need consideration. If they are unfamiliar with the way to the bathroom or even the kitchen for a glass of water (or midnight snack), a small amount of light to guide their path can make all the difference in their comfort. By avoiding obstacles they wouldn't see in the dark, they also avoid the pain of stubbing a toe!

We enjoy this same comfort in our Christian walk. Jesus, the Light of the World, enables us to walk in the Light. In doing so, we avoid obstacles in our relationships. Avoiding the pain of stumbling in the dark comes when we keep a short account of our sin with the Light himself. When we confess and forsake, He cleanses and lights our way. No more stubbed toes or fear from the looming darkness necessary.

design tip

Beautiful nightlight options abound that are more stylistic for décor,
but also the traditional plugin nightlight still works especially if you only need a temporary solution.

Thank you, my Lord and Savior and friend, for being everything my earthly friends cannot. You fulfill every longing and need, and I praise you for your love toward me.

Nothing Compares to You

"Abraham believed God, and it was credited to him as righteousness," and he was called God's friend.

JAMES 2:23

Many of us enjoy the opportunity to invite our family and friends over into our homes to enjoy meals, fellowship, and more. When we invite someone into our space, we open ourselves up for deeper intimacy and relationship than casual meetings in a restaurant or coffee shop provide. Heartfelt conversations happen within the context of our homes and living life together.

design tip

If you enjoy entertaining your friends and family, invest in beautiful plates, accessories, and tableware. Look for markdowns at the end of the seasons to stretch your dollars the farthest.

There is no comparison though to the opportunity we have for relationship with God. Abraham, a friend of God, believed the promises God made. As we grow in relationship with Him after our salvation, we can lean on His promises as well.

I Kings and Acts tell us that He knows all the hearts of mankind.

Proverbs reminds us that He is a friend who sticks closer than a brother.

Psalms teaches us that He knew us before our very conception, knows the number of hairs on our heads, and keeps our tears in a bottle.

What immeasurable comfort this truth brings even on the loneliest and most sorrow-filled days.

Today I am thankful, Lord, for the record you left us demonstrating the importance of your attention to detail and accuracy. I know I can trust you with the details of my life.

Measure Twice, Cut Once

According to all that I am going to show you, as the pattern of the tabernacle and the pattern of all its furniture, just so you shall construct it.

Exodus 25:9

Do you ever get excited about the beauty of the detail God's Word gives us in the record of the Old Testament? Reading through the Bible each year I still find nuggets of detail I haven't seen before. Take for instance the instructions given to Moses about the building of the tabernacle. The instructions are very clear with detailed measurements and requirements. The detail for the pattern of the furniture inside even had its own specifications. This reminds me of what a detail-oriented God we serve.

Precision and accuracy were important to Him, just as it is in the design of our own homes. Remember the adage, "Measure twice, cut once?" Homebuilders, designers, and decorators know the importance of taking multiple measurements to save not only money but also time. Being careful to understand the dimensions of a space and working within those dimensions from the beginning will save a lot of painstaking effort in the end.

design tip

You can't measure too much. Whether it's for a custom-sized piece or trying to decide if something is too large for a room, measure with precision and take careful notes.

this is our FARM and this is our Home

Bless THIS Home

Lord, I pray you'll keep my eyes on you so that I may walk in obedience to whatever you call me to.

I'm Building a What?

Make for yourself an ark of gopher wood; make rooms in the ark and coat it with pitch inside and out.
GENESIS 6:14

We choose design elements because they are aesthetically pleasing. Paint, wall-paper, or even shiplap can be either a beautiful background or a focal point. We choose specific décor, flooring, and countertops. All choices intended to create the form we imagined, hoping we enjoy our home's appearance upon completion.

I can't help but wonder what Noah's neighbors thought. Surely, they wondered what he was doing. Yet Noah obeyed God. God gave him the exact measurements, wood, and number of decks. Extreme specificity followed by extreme obedience. Without obedience, the ark might have sunk! God knew Noah would obey, because he had established a pattern of obedience. What an excellent reminder that when I maintain a faithful and consistent walk with God, the immense tasks He might call me to along the way won't be difficult to follow and obey. They will instead be more of the same, because I have created a pattern of obedience already.

design tip

If you're a fan of cottage and farmhouse style kitchens then try incorporating painted finds like this shabby-chic chandelier, white & wood sign, DIY chalkboard, ironstone, and greenery. The monochromatic theme is crisp and clean while offering the perfect contrast to the chalkboard and greige walls.
—Jennifer Ingram, IG @graciousspaces

Father, I thank you for the example in Scripture of the importance of giving generously to your kingdom work and I pray that as you continue to bless me, I will always keep my hands open to you.

Old Testament Bling

He engraved cherubim, lions and palm trees on the surfaces of the supports and on the panels,
in every available space, with wreaths all around.

1 Kings 7:36

Solomon took the important task of building the temple for God very seriously. The building took twenty years to complete and was a magnificent work of art. The descriptions of the wood and precious metals used in the construction fill me with awe even by today's standards. I love reading the detail in the description of the temple building as well because we even get insight into the interior décor. This verse describes angels, lions, palm trees, and wreaths. It indicates that the decorations were important and even glamorous. Many items were overlaid with gold. Solomon's style was definitely high end!

I can only imagine that Solomon spared no expense knowing that everything he possessed had been given by God. How would our devotion to the Lord look different today if we had a "no expense spared" mentality? Would we give generously of our time, energy, and even our monetary resources to further the Kingdom, for His glory?

design tip

Decorating with metallics including gold, silver, and copper remains a beautiful way to add a touch of brilliance. Small touches are massively effective so no need to gild everything you see.

Lord, I pray you will show me clearly when it's time I make a stand and go against the flow so that I may fulfill my purpose and bring you glory!

Trendy Wendy

For am I now seeking the approval of man, or of God? Or am I trying to please man?
If I were still trying to please man, I would not be a servant of Christ.

GALATIANS 1:10

Trendsetters are often ahead of their time. Forging beauty in ways that we never expected, many times early public reception can be negative. I think sometimes it's easy to get caught up in what so and so is doing to decorate this home, and what someone else is doing over here and copying a style even if it's not really you. Creatives often believe in their vision whether others applaud or not.

And in the same line of thought if we find ourselves only agreeing with and pleasing those around us by not speaking truth into their lives when they are wrong, aren't we way off track? Our purpose on this earth is not to make everyone around us happy with our decisions and choices. Rather we are here to bring God glory by making His name known. Sometimes that means we go against the flow, and maybe rock the boat a bit.

— design tip —

Don't be afraid to make some choices in your homes that may go against what others advise.
If it's something that brings you joy, it's ok to be a trendsetter.

I thank you, Father, for preparing Heaven for us one day. Nothing will compare on this earth to the beauty that awaits us and the luxury of dwelling in your presence forevermore.

Walking on Sunshine

The wall was made of jasper, and the city of pure gold, as pure as glass.

Revelation 21:18

We are attracted to beautiful things. We want the homes we live in and enjoy with our families filled with things that are lovely. But we are wise to budget in making purchases. The reality is that none of our possessions are eternal.

The Creator of the universe has prepared Heaven to be a magnificent home for us. I know that the splendor of Heaven is the very presence of the Lord in that place. But we will walk with wonder and amazement down streets of pure gold, looking at walls made of precious stones and the luxury of every good and every perfect thing around us. The Master Builder has a home prepared in Heaven waiting for us that will quite literally blow our minds and what we do on this earth will only be a tiny drop in the bucket of the magnificence that awaits us.

design tip

I am all about texture and baskets on the wall, however I love extra dimension, so I use circular placemats before I begin adding baskets. I used 3M strips and a nail to attach to the wall and then finished it off with lamb's ear and succulents.
—Caroline Bivens, www.carolinebivensdesigns.com, Insta: @c.b._designs

As David prayed, so will I. God, you are my hiding place, you preserve me from trouble and surround me with songs of deliverance.
I praise and thank you for this truth.

Safe Spaces

You are my hiding place; You preserve me from trouble; You surround me with songs of deliverance. Selah.

PSALM 32:7

Chaos and Mayhem? Refuge and Calm? Our home vacillates between both when things get busy. When I can't keep up with daily life, I start cleaning. I cleaned out a closet recently for no other reason than I needed to put my mind at ease about an expected busy season. A deadline, business trip, or heavy sports schedule, home can feel like chaos when the schedule is relentless. Planning enables me to handle those stressful feelings. Staying on top of organization or just removing clutter brings a sense of satisfaction and balance.

Just as David cried out to the Lord that He was his hiding place, we all need a place of comfort to retreat to when things are busy, difficult, or discouraging. Our homes should be that place of rest for our husbands, our children, and ourselves. Taking the time to prepare in advance benefits everyone so they still find rest in those in-between moments.

design tip

Don't be afraid to ask for help in the busy seasons. They don't last forever, but the stress can build and overwhelm. Clearing the clutter fifteen minutes at a time can be emotionally stabilizing and every little bit helps in the long run!

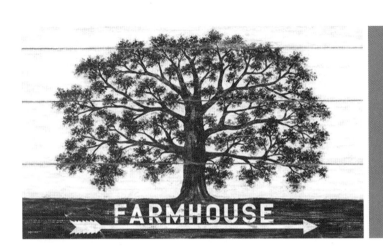

I pray, Lord, that you will help me see others as you see them, and work to remain free from bitterness as I navigate through daily life.

Let's Get to the Root of It

See to it that no one comes short of the grace of God;
that no root of bitterness springing up causes trouble.

HEBREWS 12:15

One of the mistakes people make when decorating their home comes from trying to do too much. Pinterest fueled this challenge for many of us. Many decisions regarding style are not forever. Paint, lighting fixtures, and flooring can all be changed as your needs and desires—and budget—allows. Once you begin adding in random things to your décor, it is hard to stop. Before you know it, you have a hodgepodge and no sense of order.

Bitterness can creep into hearts in much the same way. Whether it's the missed invitation to lunch with the girls, or the miscommunication over schedules with the husband, little things tend to come in and crowd out our hearts. We must live with an eye toward our tendency to hold on to those hurts and be ruthless in eliminating it from our lives. If we practice believing the best about others, I am more prone to give people grace when they hurt me.

design tip

Be intentional in your home to stay in your style. Enjoy those other things, and even plan for a future design changeup or a new home. Your style and needs will change in the different seasons of life.

As the sun sets each day, Lord, help me keep a short account of my sin with you. Remove the root of anger in my heart so that the devil has no way to gain traction in my life.

Who's Keeping Score?

Do not let the sun set upon your anger, and do not give the devil a foothold.

Ephesians 4:26-27

When building your own home, consider what direction the windows face. With a bit of elevation, windows that face either east or west provide an excellent location to view the sun. I so enjoy my quiet time in the morning watching the stars and moon disappear and the sun rise.

As the sun sets, it's appropriate to review our day. Assessing where we have fallen short, we can make a habit to keep a short account with God and each other. Many times, it's little things that accumulate like anger. The root anger is in our hearts and this is just what the devil wants. He knows he can keep us from accomplishing God's purposes in our lives and in the lives of others if he bows us down with the weight of anger.

design tip

There are two ways to paint around your windows. If you are using a saturated or bold color on your walls, using a bright white on the frame and sill can be a brilliant contrast. A subtler variation would be to paint them the same color but with a semi-gloss or gloss added for just a bit different texture.

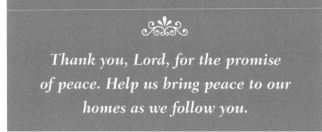

Thank you, Lord, for the promise of peace. Help us bring peace to our homes as we follow you.

Peace or Pandemonium

Peace I leave with you; my peace I give you.

JOHN 14:27A

One of the things missing in our society today is peace. We are too busy for it really. Filling every moment with something to do, somewhere to be, and no time for peace. Whether work or play, these things never satisfy. Jesus, the ultimate measure of satisfaction, promised peace to us.

Our homes should be marked by peace. We encourage peacefulness in our homes with simplicity. The colors we choose, the décor we pick, and openness of our space all contribute to the overall feeling. We invite others to sit and be at peace with us when our space is open to them. I don't live in fantasyland though. I know a color scheme doesn't stop squabbles among the young'uns or even the teenagers for that matter. I wish it would, then we could easily resolve most household problems. Let's work to make each area of our home an inviting and peaceful place for our family, friends, and even our neighbors and strangers to want to be. There's not much peace in our world today, let's work to change that in our homes.

design tip

Serenity in a bedroom can be achieved in shades of blue or green. Choosing tone on tone color from the same palette mixed with white and cream keep the calm feeling throughout the room.

Thank you, Lord, for the promise of overflowing hope and the promise of joy and peace when we trust you. Help me to live in the full power of the Holy Spirit!

Filled and Overflowing

May the God of hope fill you with all joy and peace as you trust in him,
so that you may overflow with hope by the power of the Holy Spirit.

ROMANS 15:13

Choosing the furniture and accessories that fill our homes can be an incredible delight. Seeing that vision become reality is exciting. Sometimes the decisions can be overwhelming because of the sheer magnitude choices. Not sure about blue walls? That's ok, you can change your mind next season!

When we choose to live a life of submission to Christ, we have the power of the Holy Spirit indwelling and allowing us to be filled with ALL joy and peace. Isn't that what we are ultimately seeking anyway? A life that overflows with hope and empowered by the Holy Spirit. No need for too many choices or expanding budgets, once for all Christ did the work of redemption, and we get to live life filled with joy and peace.

design tip

I love advising clients to prepare for change. Because I love change, I like my décor to have built-in versatility. I suggest buying big, expensive items in light, neutral colors. Then buy small décor, accessories, rugs, etc., with pattern and color so you can swap everything out with the seasons or your moods. I also love rearranging rooms and shopping my house for a fresh feel without spending a dime. As you can tell, I'm a practical decorator. I believe with a little creativity you can still have a lot of fun without spending a lot.
—Julie Lancia, www.thedesigntwins.com, Insta: @julie.thedesigntwins

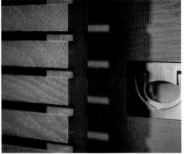

I praise you, Lord, for your compassion and unfailing love toward me. I'm am so thankful I can place my full trust and confidence in you.

Built to Last

"Though the mountains be shaken, and the hills be removed, yet my unfailing love for you will not be shaken nor my covenant of peace be removed," says the LORD, who has compassion on you.

Isaiah 54:10

We don't question if a chair will hold us when we sit down; we just sit down. A chair is designed to function in such a way that it can support our weight as we sit. Certain pieces of furniture are considered foundational elements in a room. A bedroom requires a mattress. In a living room the essential is a sofa or a group of chairs—necessary items for the room to function properly.

I'm so grateful for the compassion of the Lord. The earth can be crumbling around me, but I know that I can trust in his unfailing love. The foundation for the walk of my Christian life is that God has never and will never fail me, no matter who else does or how very bad circumstances may get. My foundation rests in the knowledge that He is unfailing and that causes me to function in the way that I was designed.

design tip

Whether you are budgeting for all new furniture or redecorating a room, be sure to put the majority of your budget dollars into the foundational pieces. The essentials should be high quality and built to last.

Thank you, Lord, for the written record of your Word, and the way it applies to us today. May I be faithful to follow and apply it.

Timeless

The grass withers and the flowers fall, but the word of our God endures forever.
ISAIAH 40:8

Some people exude style. People like Audrey Hepburn are iconic with a timeless quality. Her appeal transcends generations. Furniture can also be timeless. Styles come and go, but certain elements of style are always relevant. From platform beds to Chesterfield sofas and trestle tables, some pieces just fit into almost any décor style of the present time and place. The enduring nature of the piece causes it to be timeless.

God's word endures forever. People come and go, grass and flowers die, but God's word endures through all the ages of time and is timeless. Relevant to every generation past and every generation to come, the Word of God should be a book we are very familiar with and if we say we believe it then we should make every effort to read cover to cover. It is the way we learn who God is and what He means to us.

design tip

When it comes to picking furniture pieces for your home don't be afraid to mix the old with the new. Vintage or antique furniture that tells a story or has special memories for you adds instant character and appeal to your home while newer pieces allow you to make your own memories and connections to pass on.
—Kelly Radcliff, www.thetatteredpew.com, Insta: @thetatteredpew

I thank you, Father, for the wisdom you grant me. Help me to apply it fully to my life so that I may please you in all I do and say.

Solid Construction

By wisdom a house is built, and through understanding it is established;
through knowledge its rooms are filled with rare and beautiful treasures.

PROVERBS 24:3-4

Rooms filled with unique treasures start conversations. A recent visit to a new home caused me to ask about the enormous wood beams and unique pieces inside. The homeowner selected certain pieces specifically because of their history. They added value to the home because of their story. Without a sturdy foundation though, these beautiful things wouldn't last. A solid structure is necessary to protect from the elements and keep pests outside.

design tip

Add pieces to your home that
tell a story of who you are
as a person. My goal is to make
it warm and inviting for
our family and friends.
—Amy Stuckey,
IG @the_refinedfarmhouse

Don't you love the book of Proverbs? Chock full of the best verses for daily living, the wisdom recorded for us is essential. This verse speaks of our homes and relates it to wisdom and knowledge. I've heard it explained that wisdom was the application of knowledge—they work in tandem. Wisdom and knowledge build and fill our hearts with the essential things we should know and apply. When we act with wisdom, we apply the knowledge that we have been filling our hearts and minds with.

Thank you, Lord, for the variety you created in us. I thank you that we don't all look the same, think the same or even act the same. Help us to celebrate the things we are alike in and work together to further the kingdom.

Textural Details

So, we, though many, are one body in Christ, and individually members one of another.

ROMANS 12:5

*F*rom rough to smooth or shiny to matte, texture can add dimension and depth to our interiors. A fuzzy blanket, cozy chair, small candle, and soft lighting create warmth in a room in an inviting way. Bright colors and fun patterns with loads of tactile textures create an atmosphere of energy and fun in a playroom.

This reminds me of the body of Christ. A variety of textures—some rough, some smooth—in coordination with each other can create an atmosphere of invitation. The people we live with are a microcosm of the church at large. We know we have many differences with the people that we share our lives with 24/7. Various textures are good things and keep things interesting instead or boring and flat. Let's celebrate the differences and find ways to coordinate together to spread the message of the gospel.

— *design tip* —

My favorite design element is TEXTURE! Adding rough woods and baskets to your vignette can bring so much depth to your decor. And using things like shiplap, beadboard, and board and batten on your walls can really add richness and set the perfect backdrop for your decor!
—Jenny Zacharewicz, IG @bigfamilylittlefarmhouse

May I follow, dear Lord, the clear teaching that Psalms record for me. Help me stand guard in this very important and potentially destructive area.

The Eyes Have It

I will set no wicked thing before mine eyes.

PSALM 101:3A

Windows create a beautiful architectural element in a home. Sunlight streams in, bathing our rooms in beautiful natural light. A gorgeous view beyond the windows can be enjoyed while indoors doing other tasks and, as a bonus, staying away from pesky mosquitos. Yes, I do live in the south! I adore a home with large windows; it just feels spacious. Windows also keep the bad stuff out: bugs, rain, and even the cold draft of winter or hot steamy air of midsummer.

I've heard it said eyes are the windows to the soul. If we wish to walk with integrity and behave wisely, we must be intentional about the things we allow into our lives. Being vigilant of what we allow in our homes and in front of our eyes is something that we must monitor daily. If there is something in our homes or hearts that prevents us from following David's example, we should be careful to remove it.

design tip

If you decide to use curtains or drapes on floor-size windows, be sure to have drapes hit the floor.

If you are unsure of length to order always go one size longer to be on the safe side.

You can always get them hemmed when you have them in hand.

Lord, help me trust when the answers aren't the ones I want
and submit my will to yours. Give me grace to endure and faith
to believe when the days are long and hard.

Doesn't Feel Good!

And we know that all things work together for good to those who love God.

ROMANS 8:28

Certain elements pull together to create a harmonious home. Pieces that on their own may not be interesting or special, but because of the repetition, color or shape throughout the home create rhythm which is essential to symmetry. Symmetry provides harmony and therefore peaceful transition from room to room.

Harmony and peace aren't guaranteed for the Christian. You know that no matter how closely you walk with the Lord, trials and difficulties come. These things aren't good themselves. When we pray for a certain outcome and God replies no, it can be difficult to trust that all things will work together. What we must do is trust the Designer, the one who knows beginning from end, to know that the overall composition of our lives will flow in harmony and work together for our good and His glory.

design tip

A large piece of art or massive mirror isn't required to anchor a wall over a sofa. Instead you can group several items that together create a gallery. While it is simpler to create a symmetrical balance with equal sizes and shapes, asymmetrical balance can also be visually interesting and exciting. Don't be afraid to play with the arrangement until it feels right.

Lord, I thank you today that you coordinate all the parts in our families. Help us to be obedient to play the role you have given us.

No I in Team

I planted, Apollos watered, but God gave the growth. So, neither he who plants nor he who waters is anything, but only God who gives the growth.

I Corinthians 3:6,7

If you've ever participated in group sports, sung in a choir, or decorated a home you know that it is all about the team. It requires a massive team effort to get a home prepared for a homeowner. Sometimes special equipment must be rented to move furniture into locations with difficult access. After furniture placement, the real effort to bring it all together begins with the various wall hangings, mirrors, and accessories.

Our homes operate as a team in very similar fashion. If you have more than one person living in your home, you know that the things don't get done unless everyone pitches in and plays their part. Understanding that we are all important in service to the kingdom of God helps us when we might feel underappreciated or unnecessary. We all have a part to play. We might need to plant the seed, but that doesn't mean we will get to see the fruit of that work. We trust God to provide that in due time.

design tip

A subtle change to consider is to paint your ceiling a lighter shade of your wall color. This really makes a space feel brighter and more spacious.

Help me to always choose to be joyful, no matter my circumstances, dear Lord. As you work your purposes in me, help me to be a willing vessel molded by the trials you allow.

If I Fits, I Sits

Count it all joy, my brothers, when you meet trials of various kinds,
for you know that the testing of your faith produces steadfastness.

JAMES 1:2

It can feel like days of trial and difficulty sometimes when you are designing or re-designing a home. There are long hours and frustration, especially when someone orders something wrong. Sofas that don't fit through doorways, finishes in the wrong shade of brown, and other errors on the job can be time consuming and expensive. But perseverance always wins in the end. The job reaches completion eventually and there is joy and delight in the finished product.

One day we will be a finished product too. The idea of counting it as joy, the process of stepping back and evaluating our situation through the lens of God's Word and eternity seems outlandish and yet that's precisely what we must do. We may never understand why certain things happen this side of heaven, but we can rest in the knowledge that we are being strengthened and fit for service in the days ahead.

design tip

If you would like your room to appear to have much higher ceilings, keep in mind that the scale of your furniture can assist. Low back chairs combined with tall mirrors can create an illusion of height.

Thank you, Lord, for the record of Creation and the attention to detail. I praise you for your awesome power and might.

Whales, Anemones, and Platypuses, Oh my!

*By the seventh day God had finished the work he had been doing;
so on the seventh day he rested from all his work.*

<small>GENESIS 2:2</small>

Our master Designer not only created the whale but also the anemone, not only the warthog but also the platypus, and He created you and me. When we read the account of the Creation in Scripture, we are given rich details for the daily changes on the blank canvas. As you contemplate the enormity of Creation, you will be filled with awe and wonder. From concept to creation to future purpose all at one time.

I think about the finishing touches of Creation and am reminded how each home requires finishing touches. In no way am I saying you must spend a fortune to "finish" your home. Finishing could be as simple as a fresh candle, a new set of sheets, and a soft blanket. Finishing might be getting rid of excess stuff and clutter and doing a fresh dusting and vacuum. I hope you get the picture. It doesn't have to be grand to be thoughtful.

— design tip —

The idea behind the finishing touch is less to do with the item and more to do with the thought behind the act. The stack of fresh towels, a new bar of soap, and extra shampoo and conditioner for the guest in your home. Little touches make our home a haven.

Thank you, Lord, for the blessing of seeing rewards from our hard work. Help me to remember to teach these lessons to my children and others you put in my life to influence.

Clean Out the Stalls

Where there are no oxen, the manger is clean, but abundant crops come by the strength of the ox.

PROVERBS 14:4

I know you are probably wondering where I'm going with this, but bear with me a minute. The truth in this verse is rich. We raised sheep for several years. Let me tell you, the barn is NOT clean when you have livestock. The reminder here is that we reap benefits because of the hard work of the ox. No work, no reward. If we are not willing to put in the work, we cannot expect to benefit.

This principle plays out in our homes. For things to run well and look good, everyone must play their part. Keeping a home maintained and clean is part of the job that must be done. Being good stewards of the home God gives us means we take care of the needs and required upkeep. When we want new things like a sofa or a bed, we may have to take on extra work to afford the new item, or if it's a whole home design job, it may be a new job or a sacrifice in some other budget category.

design tip

Once we acquire new things, taking care of them demonstrates good stewardship. Important lessons to pass on to our children when they are young.

Father help me
to keep the
proper perspective
on all you've
given me.
Help me to
keep my hands and
my doors open
in service to you.

Hosting Angels

Do not neglect to show hospitality to strangers, for by this some have entertained angels without knowing it.

HEBREWS 13:2

A home that is inviting communicates warmth and openness to others. Neighbors and strangers alike should be welcome guests. Unfortunately, overwhelmed schedules create difficulty in finding a spare moment to entertain. But that isn't God's intention or plan for our lives. I am encouraged to find time to be intentional and reconnect with friends, but to also look for opportunities to bless strangers by opening our home. Having guests sometimes means being ready at a moment's notice, so the habit of a tidy house helps. But sometimes it just isn't possible. We have entertained with laundry to be folded…on the sofa. I have thrown things in the bedroom at the last moment and shut the door. Keeping priorities, I must devote time to others.

What holds you back from being more open? A proper perspective that everything belongs to God will help us overcome any unwillingness to use our home as a place to show love to others.

design tip

There are seasons when the schedule overwhelms us. If we are to have open homes for family and guests alike, we may need to ask for help. Whether we exchange services with another person or pay someone to come in to help with the upkeep, I do believe it's an important concession to make.

Lord, I pray that the Holy Spirit will fill my heart and my mouth so that others will see the difference you make in me.

Build It Up or Tear It Down

A gentle tongue is a tree of life, but perverseness in it breaks the spirit.

PROVERBS 15:4

While there are many fine mediums for artistic endeavors like metal, glass, and composites, wood is still probably the number one resource for furniture, wall art, and accessories. Grain appearance, durability, and strength are all factors in development of these pieces.

When we are tired and weary from the daily grind, we are tempted to allow our tongue free rein hurting those we love the most. A gentle tongue, considered a tree of life, can sometimes be a challenge. A gentle tongue sounds different, doesn't it? I mean you don't have to go far to hear harsh words and even if you don't hear the exact words, you can tell by the tone that it's not gentleness being employed. May we work to be a tree of life, wise, and uplifting to those around us, even when we don't want to be. We will show Christ's love when we choose to speak differently. This change will come as we continue to submit our hearts to His leadership and allow the Holy Spirit to work in us.

design tip

If you are considering new flooring, a contrasting wood stain keeps your furniture from blending in. You can go lighter or darker, but choosing a different color helps break up monotony.

*Lord, light up our homes and
our world with your love. Help me to
do my part to spread the news of the
Gospel and the light we so desperately
need to quell the darkness.*

Light It Up!

I am the light of the world. Whoever follows me will not walk in darkness but will have the light of life.

JOHN 8:12

After color and style one of the most necessary decisions is lighting. With a remodel or build, lighting decisions need to be made early because of the electrical considerations. An even illumination source, ambient lighting creates sustainable light when there is no source for natural light. A chandelier, track lights, or ceiling and wall mounted fixtures can be employed to assist. Recessed lighting and down lights illuminate a space without being in your line of sight when not in use. If it's not a complete build or remodel and the lighting doesn't meet your needs, table lamps and floor lamps can be used to help with lighting.

Just as we need lighting in our homes, our hearts need to be illuminated by Jesus. He said He is the light, and He is all we need. Our world needs to know that Jesus is the only thing that will meet their darkest and deepest needs. The answer for the problems we face today is Jesus, only Jesus.

design tip

When decorating a room, aim to create different levels of lighting. Consider lighting backsplashes, paintings, and cabinet interiors as well as the usual overhead and table lighting choices.

*Help me, Lord, keep my eye on the truth of your word. I long to stay
focused on the task you have for me, keep me faithful!*

Shine a Light on Me

For the commandment is a lamp and the teaching a light, and the reproofs of discipline are the way of life.

PROVERBS 6:23

Task lighting is an essential for many rooms, especially an office and the kitchen. Task lighting brings focused light to a particular task. Good quality task lighting not only brightens the spot where you are working, but also increases contrast so that our eyes don't have to work so hard to differentiate between items. In the kitchen task lighting assists as we meal prep or wash dishes. In an office, it's helpful when working on the computer or writing a letter or paying a bill. In a cozy corner with a comfortable chair or chaise a task light can make it much easier to read.

The Bible itself is our task light. The whole counsel of God containing reproof, encouragement, and commands. Filled with stories of overwhelming victory and stunning defeat and tales of the highs and lows of many heroes of our faith. Being careful to fill our hearts with the entirety of God's word can help us avoid many pitfalls in life that we can go through.

design tip

Under cabinet lights are one of the nicest finishing touches in a kitchen. Being able to use the entire counter space with the addition of these simple lights is a game changer!

Father, as I walk with You, help me to overflow with your light and draw others' eyes to you. Help them long to know you because they see You in me.

Hocus Focus

In the same way, let your light shine before others, so that they may see your good works and give glory to your Father who is in heaven.

MATTHEW 5:16

We acquire certain treasures over time that we want to draw special attention to. Whether it's a wedding portrait, a sculpture or a piece of wall art, we love beautiful things and we work to ensure that they have a spot of importance in our homes. Depending on its location, it may need an accent light. Various lights exist that help us focus attention to these special pieces.

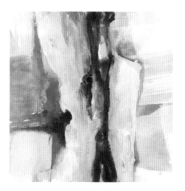

Our purpose should be to draw all attention to Christ. The things we do and say should always, first and foremost, be intended to bring glory and honor to Him. This is our primary purpose and reason for being here on this earth. We are to bring a focus to Him, just as we might that precious piece of art or special gift. If we are working to gain all the attention for ourselves and our achievements, we might need to take a step back and reevaluate those priorities. It's always and only all about Him.

design tip

Don't discount the value of a dimmer switch. It's an easy way to control the light, saves electricity, and even the life expectancy of the bulb.

Thank you, Lord, that you offer mercy and grace in my need.
I praise you that I can come boldly into your presence
no matter where or when!

Quit Pretending

Let us therefore come boldly to the throne of grace,
that we may obtain mercy and find grace to help in time of need.

HEBREWS 4:16

Keeping the proper proportion in a room involves a clear understanding of the way that scale and proportion work together to accomplish the look of the whole. Sometimes features that are not in proportion can't be changed because of the architecture, but they can be disguised creatively with paint, draperies, and furniture.

I am so relieved that when challenges in my life arise, I don't have to disguise or pretend they aren't there. Rather this verse reminds me to come boldly. No hiding in guilt and shame through errors of my own failures and sinfulness. No pressure to perform when I'm weary and laid low, and no lack of compassion to be found when life just gets hard. Grace and mercy in abundant supply when I need it the most.

design tip

If you are trying to disguise a small window on a large wall, you might paint the wall a darker color in effect making it smaller. Add curtains or draperies that aren't for that size window by putting the hardware on the outside of the window and up much higher on the wall. This easy disguise plays with the proportion in a room that has challenges.

*Thank you,
Father,
for the
promise
of heaven.
Thank you
for the joy
that we know
we will have
and help us
choose joy
while we walk
this earth.*

Holy Presence

You make known to me the path of life; in your presence there is fullness of joy;
at your right hand are pleasures forevermore.

PSALM 16:11

The promise of Heaven with the presence of Christ for the rest of our days fills me with such gratefulness. The joy that we will know there will make every experience here pale in comparison. We will have the lasting joy of being home, never more to roam. To always have the visual presence of Christ before us and with us and all around us.

As much as we try to make our homes a place of joy and comfort, nothing compares to what He has stored up for us in glory. Cultivating a heart and home that is known for joy should be our desire here on earth. While it will never match Heaven, we can do our best to create a haven. A place that, while not perfect, is based in joy and care for each other and love. We can add all the right colors, keep the design rules, but at the end of the day if there is no joy in our walls, it will be for nothing.

design tip

As you place accessories like candles, vases, etc., be sure to choose odd numbers in your groupings. It is more appealing than an even number.

*Lord, I thank you
today that
as I walk in daily
relationship
with you, you in turn
fill my heart with
desires that align
with your will.
Keep me close to you.*

Asking and Receiving

And this is the confidence that we have toward him,
that if we ask anything according to his will he hears us.

1 John 5:14

Hiring a designer for a décor job is a wise move. A professional understands construction, coordination of pieces, and timetables, and will give perspective from experience and education. An expert will answer your requests with honesty and reality. One might tell you no because of the expense, time involved, or it's not best for your home. When the things we ask for fit the vision, they will work to figure out how to incorporate your ideas. After all, they want a happy customer!

Our master designer knows the plan for our lives. When we pray according to His will He hears us. We can be sure we are praying in His will when we make a practice of walking with Him daily. His word filling our hearts and minds, fills us with the desires that we have and pray for.

design tip

Make wise choices in selecting furniture for the season of life you are currently in. A white living room with littles can be a nightmare to keep clean, and, honestly, they still find the sharpie markers.
They are only little for a short time. Save yourself a lot of headaches and be patient.

*Lord, keep me focused on reaching
others for the Kingdom in my choices
and convict me of my selfishness when
I'm inwardly focused instead.*

It's Not About You

If a brother or sister is poorly clothed and lacking in daily food, and one of you says to them,
"Go in peace, be warmed and filled," without giving them the things needed for the body, what good is that?
So also, faith by itself, if it does not have works, is dead.

JAMES 2:15-17

Our most recent home purchase was a home that was far larger than we felt we needed. In a way only God can do He made it abundantly clear that this was indeed the home for us. The only conclusion we had was that He intended for us to keep it open for church functions and those in need. Providing opportunities to gather and grow should be an important part of our decision making in home décor.

Designing our homes intentionally to be ready at a moment's notice to meet needs should be our purpose. Being willing and available to meet physical and emotional needs gives us the opportunity to meet their ultimate need—their spiritual need of knowing Christ.

design tip

In choosing throw and accent pillows for your chairs and sofa, don't settle for a single pair. Multiple pairs and sizes add interest to a solid sofa. Remember too that switching out pillows in different seasons can give a room a different look altogether.

Lord, thank you for the reminder to rest in your power and grace to live in harmony with each other.

Sing Me a Song

May the God of endurance and encouragement grant you to live in such harmony with one another, in accord with Christ Jesus.

Romans 15:5

Décor in a home creates a composition just as a musician composes a piece of music. Composition literally means an arrangement of elements in artistic form. When the placing of décor in our home is harmonious it just "feels right." Our homes have a group of elements as well—the people living in the home—and, honestly, when each is working together and in tandem with the other it is indeed a harmonious place to dwell, isn't it?

I love how Paul reminds us that God grants us the opportunity to live in harmony with one another. It's a gift of grace and he reminds us in the verse that He is the God of endurance and encouragement, because often we need that as well, right? If your heart is out of harmony, return to the source and let him fill your heart with the harmony you seek.

design tip

I love to decorate a space with light shades of furniture with classic, clean lines and add in bold accents that I can change out throughout the year according to the season. I use this system to bring in pops of color I'm loving at the time through things like pillows, throw blankets, vases, greenery, and flowers.
—Jenny Caspers, www.acleanprismlife.com, Insta: @acleanprismlife

I trust you,
Lord, to
continue
working on
me. I ask you
to take the
edges of my
heart and
soften and
mold them to
look like you.

LET'S *stay* HOME

Trash to Treasure

It is better to dwell in the corner of the housetop, than with a brawling woman and in a wide house.

PROVERBS 25:24

A unified and harmonious room can be felt easier than it can be explained. When the piece,furniture, lamp, or accessory, is right you just know it. Good designers have a sense about certain items and finding just the right piece for a spot is the key to a harmonious union.

As I think about harmony though, I can't help but think about this reminder in Proverbs. Our attitude as women is integral to the overall composition of the home. It doesn't matter how fine your furniture is, or how gorgeous your décor, if you are a contentious and angry woman, there is no one on earth who will want to live there with you. And you know what, you have the choice. Holy Spirit powered living means letting go of that cantankerous ugly spirit and letting the Lord soften and buff your rough edges.

design tip

This vintage mail sorter was a splurge, and it didn't even fit in my house. I just had to have it though. Simplifying its purpose by making drawers for the 35 cubbies, it has become a beautiful statement piece. Sometimes finding unusual pieces that are out of the box become some of the greatest décor pieces.
—Caroline Bivens, www.carolinebivensdesigns.com, Insta: @c.b._designs

A Place to Rest

Let us make a little chamber, I pray thee, on the wall; and let us set for him there a bed, and a table, and a stool, and a candlestick.

II Kings 4:10

Traveling as an international missionary evangelist, my dad stays with many churches and individuals who have space based on this passage in II Kings. The record here indicates that the Shunammite woman and her husband gave their best because they knew Elisha was a man of God. They thought through what his other needs might be, a table and chair and even a candlestick. A nice extra touch to make him comfortable as he passed through.

My heart must also open in invitation for the Holy Spirit's guidance. If this is my heart's desire, it needs to be kept free of the clutter of the sins of pride, lust, deceit, ingratitude, dare I continue? When I am careful to weed out the trash and mess, I can have an open dwelling for my Savior to rule my heart and mind and an open invitation to make Himself at home there.

design tip

One of the finishing touches that can pull a room together is a rug. When you've got a lot of legs in various wood tones, give them common ground with an area rug. A rug also helps to create a soothing transition between the furniture and the wood floor.

LOVE

makes this house a home

HAVE Faith

My refuge, dear Lord, is found only in you.
Keep me under the shadow of your wing as
I learn to dwell in your presence.

Here to Dwell

Because you have made the LORD your dwelling place—the Highest, who is my refuge—
no evil shall be allowed to befall you, no plague come near your tent.

PSALMS 91:9-10

We trust God as our refuge when we dwell in His shelter. What a delight to place our complete faith in the sovereign hands of the Lord. As we release full trust in the Lord, He offers protection from the flesh and the devil and all the forces of evil he can hurl in our direction. This protection is predicated though on our choice. We must first dwell and abide. The place we spend our time is where our hearts dwell.

We love to beautify our homes and make them enjoyable to come home to not only for ourselves but our family, our friends, and our guests. Each choice, from color to fabrics and finishes needs to support our goal of creating a place our family and friends decide to dwell. Our home should be a refuge from the outside world.

design tip

Are people comfortable in your home? Do they feel welcome or do they feel like they are intruding? Be sure to have at least one area that you can sit with friends and your family that is comfortable, clean, and calm. Keep coffee, lemonade, and an easy snack available for last minute drop-ins.

Thank you, Lord, that your Word is living and relevant in all seasons of my life. No matter how many times I read it, I learn and understand new things as the Holy Spirit does His work in me.

Fit for The King

But Christ as a son over his own house; whose house are we.

HEBREWS 3:6

The verses almost leapt off the page for me, the beauty of the words of the builder, the house, and the comparison of Moses and Christ and in turn our comparison to being Christ's house. He is the ultimate builder and designer, and we are his construction!

If I ever wondered about this book being of value to real Bible study and biblical principle, this passage really drove home to me that the reason for this project was firmly in God's hands. Don't you see, sister, in the same way we enjoy beautiful details and delight in finding the perfect piece or treasure that must come home with us, He delights in doing for us? The power of the Holy Spirit as he places in us the beautiful treasures of love and joy. Oh, do you see it yet? He is masterfully designing us for good works to bring him all the glory. As we submit to his Lordship, we begin to see the beautiful workmanship come together.

design tip

Don't be afraid to mix metallics in your design. It's fun to have gold and silver combined, but you can also soften their effect by adding softer textures like velvet and wool.

Lord, you are the focal point of my life.
I am sorry for the times that I make it something else;
keep my eyes on you.

Everything, Always

Looking unto Jesus, the author and finisher of our faith.

HEBREWS 12:2

*E*ach room needs a clear place of emphasis or focal point. The eye will feel restless if there is no obvious place to land. One main point of interest doesn't negate variety in detail or design. Rather, having a focal point gives us a sense of overall structure and an inherent sense of calm.

The singular point, the focal point of our heart and mind, an intentional and well-designed view of Jesus. He, who not only authored but finished, the beginning and the end, the Alpha and Omega, the first and last, the one and only Jesus knew what it would mean to endure the cross. He knew the loss of relationship in those moments as sin dwelt on his soldiers on the cross, endured it all for you and for me. He deserves nothing less than full and complete devotion. The focus of every single area of my life. All the ambition, the ideas, the passions, the desire of my heart and yours, my sister, should be to Him alone. For his glory alone. In all things. Always.

design tip

In choosing your focal point be sure to view it from all angles. Look across rooms including across from doors. With this wider perspective, you'll find the best location for your focal point.

What a gift it is that you created pleasure for us.
Thank you, Father, for the gifts of our senses to enjoy life around us.
Help me to savor your goodness to us.

Comfort Food

Taste and see that the Lord is good.
PSALM 34:8

We've heard it said that the kitchen is the heart of the home. In many ways I believe this can be true, especially if you have an area where the family can sit, congregate, or dwell together. Some of the sweetest times happen in our home around the dinner table or in preparation for that dinner. It is increasingly more difficult to make that time happen though, isn't it? Hectic lives and schedules prevent that family time more and more and having more than one child can exacerbate that exponentially.

I love how the psalmist tells us to taste and see that the Lord is good. It's an interesting choice of words to me. I think of savoring something delicious. The pleasurable act of joy. While encouraging us, he tells us to taste and see that the Lord is good. Just as in our homes, we may enjoy good Southern comfort food, how much MORE do we enjoy His goodness to us. May we savor Him today.

— *design tip* —

Entertaining doesn't require expensive dishes and tableware. Many beautiful treasures can be found by antiquing or online resales. Mix various patterns to create a unique collection that is far more interesting than a new set.

Thank you, Lord, for the gift of variety in the body of Christ.
Help me to look for ways to work with others as
we seek to spread the Gospel.

Learned Coordination

Only let your manner of life be worthy of the gospel of Christ…I may hear of you that you are standing firm in one spirit, with one mind striving side by side for the faith of the gospel.

Philippians 1:27

Complementary colors work together easily. A complementary color comes from the opposite side of the color wheel but creates a perfect contrast having one dominant color with a contrasting accent color.

Working together in our homes and our churches requires unity of purpose. But unity doesn't mean we look or talk the same. Instead our purpose of spreading the gospel to the world unites us together. This overflow in our homes could spread to our church body and then outward again to a world who needs to know Jesus. If our lives and homes don't look different to our neighbors, friends, and loved ones, then they will never want what we have. Let's not miss an opportunity to demonstrate the difference Christ makes in our lives and then seamlessly work with the rest of the body.

design tip

Blending neutrals into a complementary color scheme will keep the two colors from being overwhelming. Also keep the lighter of the two colors as your base color and use the coordinating color as an accent for interesting pops of color.

Thank you, Lord, for creating in me a heart that longs for you. Have your will and way in my life and craft a heart that will accomplish your purpose in me.

Quality Craftsmanship

For we are His workmanship, created in Christ Jesus for good works,
which God prepared beforehand so that we would walk in them.

Ephesians 2:10

If you enjoy a timeless style, you know that the quality of the build is incredibly important. You might collect timeless furniture because you want to pass it on to the next generation, or you appreciate the work involved in crafting the piece. We expect to pay more for these pieces because of the quality of construction and design.

His unique workmanship, He prepared and knew before time began what our role would be in bringing Him glory on this earth. Let that settle in your mind for a minute. His workmanship, the master Builder and Creator, created in Christ Jesus, the ultimate sacrifice who paid the highest price for us. Are you struck like I am that I don't always live up to the quality He created in me? Just as quality furniture requires quality materials and builders, we are created in the image of God, and were bought with the highest price.

---

design tip

Not every piece of furniture needs to be of utmost quality. But certain pieces—foundational ones—need to be built to last and feel special. Select certain furniture pieces with that in mind.

Lord, I pray that our homes will honor you as we seek to please you and follow your way for us.

Structural Integrity

Likewise, wives, be subject to your own husbands, so that even if some do not obey the word,
they may be won without a word by the conduct of their wives,
when they see your respectful and pure conduct.

I Peter 3:1-2

Marks of quality indicate good design. The quality of the materials used in fabric and finish but also the structure of the piece. While trends are enjoyable and artistic endeavors create new and delightful designs, solid construction and style are timeless and standard. There will always be a market for quality.

This passage reminds me that our homes are also places of quality. A home without a solid structure built into a strong foundation can't be expected to stand the test of time. When we begin our families on our wedding day, it's probably the easiest day our marriage will face. It only gets more difficult from there, my friends! Sin, the flesh, and the devil want to destroy our marriages and our homes affecting our families for generations. Following the structure God has designed for our hearts and our homes places the design on a strong foundation—the rock Jesus Christ.

---

design tip

While many of us espouse neutrals in decorating, adding pops of color can keep things visually interesting. Bookcases, mantels, ceilings, and hallways are perfect places to add accent colors.

Lord, thank you so much for the colors of Creation and the variety of shades you created. Thank you that we can all play a part in coordinating together to build the Kingdom.

Botanical Invasion

Therefore I, the prisoner of the Lord, implore you to walk in a manner worthy of the calling with which you have been called, with all humility and gentleness, with patience, showing tolerance for one another in love, being diligent to preserve the unity of the Spirit in the bond of peace.

<small>EPHESIANS 4:1-3</small>

Decorating with floral and botanical prints remains a strong way to bring color and freshness indoors. Creation's combination of colors and shades is a wonderful palette for us to duplicate. Plants have various shades of green. All the shades unify to create a beautiful landscape. Does it look disorganized or chaotic? No, instead it's a beautiful design unified by its imitation of nature.

I love how Paul reminds us that when we walk with humility, gentleness, patience, and tolerance we preserve the unity of the spirit in the bond of peace. Being united by Christ and the peace he brings us, places us in the unique opportunity to be able to demonstrate grace. Just like the colors of nature all unify to create a beautiful landscape, we create a beautiful picture of family with the various people and talents in the body.

design tip

Floral and botanical prints are wonderful as wall art and textiles.
The feel of nature is comforting and clean.

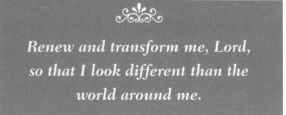

Renew and transform me, Lord, so that I look different than the world around me.

The Ultimate Flip

And do not be conformed to this world, but be transformed by the renewing of your mind.

ROMANS 12:2A

Purchasing a fixer-upper in need of renovation and transformation can be the ultimate experience for a "do it yourselfer." A home or piece of furniture might have to be stripped down to the very barest of bones to begin again. This process requires an enormous amount of work, money, and a certain amount of skill or willingness to learn the skills necessary to transform the mess before us.

God desires to transform us! Presenting our bodies as a living sacrifice to God, we ask Him to use his vast resources, labor of love, and skill to transform or renovate our minds so that we may know what His will is for our lives. In our own power, we will quickly run out of resources, skill, and strength to accomplish what He desires in us. Instead yielding all our rights and not allowing the world to influence our lives any longer creates in us the vessel useful in His service.

design tip

Shop your own home! Before I ever head out to the store to buy something new to decorate our home with I always shop my own home first (and sometimes my mom's and my sister's as well!). Just moving décor or furniture items from one spot to another gives them new life, as well as the space a new look.

—Kelly Radcliff, www.thetatteredpew.com, Insta: @thetatteredpew

Lord, I thank you for the comfort of knowing that you know me so personally and care for me deeply.

God Is in the Details

Are not two sparrows sold for a penny? Yet not one of them will fall to the ground outside your Father's care. And even the very hairs of your head are all numbered. So don't be afraid; you are worth more than many sparrows.

MATTHEW 10:29-31

The final detail work required to finish a design job can be exhausting. Without clear notes, the very last touches might be completely forgotten. The quote "God is in the details" has been attributed to Ludwig Mies van der Rohe when he was designing buildings in the mid-1900s. But it's those little things, the tiny minutia of detail, that ultimately make beautiful houses.

It's also the detail with which our Father cares for us. Think about how many pieces of hair you pulled off your own head today, and then realize that He knows how many hairs you have on your head. You. Not a collective you. You personally. He knows the number of hairs you have left today. I've pulled a couple today, how about you? He knows. He sees. He cares. If He knows when the sparrows fall, He knows when you have a need. He is the ultimate caring and loving Father. What a comfort!

design tip

Backlighting and uplighting are two interesting ways to add attention to detail. A light just below or even behind an accent wall can add depth and warmth to an environment.

Lord, use me to make a difference in this world. Open my eyes, my heart, and my hands to be generous with others who need a touch of your love.

Proper Proportions

"Give, and it will be given to you."

Luke 6:38

Knowing the size and measurements of the space you are working in is vital. Even if you are not redecorating an entire room, knowing the measurements of a dresser or bed helps to decide what to place on the wall over it. Too small a piece and it will be dwarfed by the size of the foundational item. Too large a piece and the proportion will be a distraction to everyone who enters.

Luke reminds us to be givers. And because we are givers we will have given back to us. We are reminded that the standard of measure we use will be measured back to us in return. Giving generously should mark our lives. As Christians we should be openhanded with all our resources. This doesn't necessarily refer to money either. It could be any of our resources: home, time, abilities, etc. When we give generously we should do it without any thought of getting in return, but rather we give because we have been given so much.

design tip

Creating a space that functions as it should not only helps you today, but also adds value when you are ready to sell in the future. Many of us will not remain in the same home forever.

DO EVERYTHING IN

Love

this is us

OUR LIFE OUR STORY
OUR HOME

As the Creator of our bodies and emotions, I thank you,
Lord, that you seek connection with us in these ways.
Feeling known and loved is such a comfort.

All the Feelings

And because ye are sons, God hath sent forth the Spirit of his Son into your hearts, crying, Abba, Father.

GALATIANS 4:6

As a parent, the love and care we provide to our children is vital. The time we take to provide a comforting environment and warmth of home is for the express purpose of making our house a home. I do understand our world is broken and not everyone has a home like this. For that I am so very sorry that the brokenness has touched you.

I'd like to offer hope and encouragement no matter what your earthly home held for you. Our Heavenly Father, to whom we cry Abba, is close at hand. Abba is a personal and intimate connection with the Almighty. As the children of God, we not only have the intellectual understanding that Holy God is our Father and we are his children through the beautiful process of adoption into his family at salvation, BUT we are also told in this passage that we can feel this process emotionally. The Holy Spirit communicates with our spirit and connects us emotionally to the One who knows us the best and cares for us the most.

design tip

Layering colors, patterns, and textures adds an element of comfort to a room.
From curtains to textiles and even wall art, these touches communicate relaxation.

I thank you, Lord, today for the indwelling power of the Holy Spirit. I long to live a life of holiness so that I may walk in your power and might.

Sanctuary Space

And what agreement hath the temple of God with idols? for ye are the temple of the living God; as God hath said, I will dwell in them, and walk in them; and I will be their God, and they shall be my people.

II Corinthians 6:16

A dwelling is traditionally defined as a house or living space. As we fluff and primp may we always remember that these earthly spaces are not nearly as important as our heavenly one. Creating a home of comfort and sanctuary often means removing things that are harmful or have outlived their purpose and keeping only the things that make our loved ones feel "at home."

Paul reminds us in this passage that as the Old Testament Scriptures proclaimed wherever God dwells that becomes His temple. Further study of that word is that of "sanctuary"—the holiest part of the temple. We are the temple. We should walk in obedience to his principles and live holy lives in reverence and respect to the One who indwells us.

design tip

Mixing patterns can be dangerous territory. But the reality is that using small amounts of different patterns combined with solids can add layers of interest to a collection. Just remember that small doses are the important part.

Lord, draw me close and keep me at your feet. I pray that you'll keep me humbly in your presence and dwelling in communion with you so that I will please you with my life.

Beside Still Waters

Surely goodness and mercy shall follow me all the days of my life,
and I shall dwell in the house of the LORD forever.

PSALM 23:6

illed with beautiful imagery of the Lord as our Shepherd and the comfort He provides Psalm 23 is familiar to many of us. We long to meet the needs of those who come through our doors. Basic necessities are all within our power and budgets. As my own children grow and begin new lives, my desire is for them to want to return home as often as possible, not only because their needs are met here but also because they enjoy our company.

My understanding of this passage is that not only do we yearn for our homes in Heaven, but while we are here on earth, we desire to be continually in God's presence. To sit at his feet in communion and connection. The context of the word dwell here is the idea of a return. We return and abide in Christ's presence because all our needs are met here—at His feet.

— *design tip* —

In the dining room,
use a chandelier above the table,
but keep the wattage low.
Adding table lamps to the buffet,
or a set of matching sconces on
the wall adds indirect lighting and
keeps the mood relaxed.

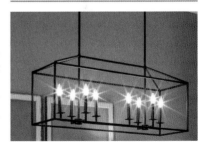

> *Beautiful Savior,*
> *thank you for*
> *the gift of beauty*
> *not only in your*
> *Creation but*
> *also in yourself.*
> *Thank you that you*
> *allow us to enjoy*
> *beautiful things.*

Beautiful Things

One thing have I desired of the LORD, that will I seek after; that I may dwell in the house of the LORD all the days of my life, to behold the beauty of the LORD, and to inquire in his temple.

PSALM 27:4

Do you enjoy beautiful things? You might be one of those rare people who don't really care, but I think that most of us are drawn to beauty. We don't pick out a piece of furniture or choose a paint color because it's ugly and unattractive. Of course, beauty is in the eye of the beholder, so some of us might have questionable tastes after all!

Isn't it lovely in reading the description here about dwelling in the house of Lord that he includes the reasoning that we can behold His beauty. Jehovah, our Creator and Maker, is beautiful. Not just in nature or character, but also in the eye of the beholder! This one thing is needful for us—abiding in his presence, not as a guest but as family. Constant communion only occurs as we remain in His presence. We demonstrate this priority by the time we dedicate to it.

design tip

Accessories and art that imitate nature remain popular. Creation is filled with beautiful things, and we should take advantage of the opportunity to duplicate them in our interiors.

You are incomparable, oh God! Your glory is too wonderful and there are not enough words to express it. Thank you, Lord, for the constant availability of your presence.

Incomprehensible

Many, O LORD my God, are the wonders which You have done,
And Your thoughts toward us; There is none to compare with You.

PSALM 40:5

aking our house a home involves finding comfortable things. Each room becomes an opportunity to invite our family and friends into our presence. Bedrooms are such a personal space, and some of my favorite conversations with my children through the years have occurred here. They will sit on the bed and start talking. If my door is closed or my space too cluttered for them to sit briefly, they won't knock, they won't come in, and they won't stay for that conversation.

God has done great wonders and has knowledge of my deepest thoughts, hurts, triumphs, and even my tears. His door is always open, and he is never too busy to hear from me. May we offer the same respite in our homes as He has given us.

design tip

Comfortable bed linens, blankets, and comforters or duvets are not inexpensive. This is one area that I do believe the extra dollars are worthwhile. Look for items you love, and then watch for sales. It's possible even with high-end textiles to get them at a discount if you watch closely enough.

Thank you, Lord, for the promise to answer our call when we are careful to seek you. I praise you Lord for your faithfulness and love to me.

Captivity

You will seek Me and find Me when you search for Me with all your heart.

JEREMIAH 29:13

Sometimes we find ourselves in a home that we don't love. I've been there. After a particularly difficult trial, we found ourselves renting an older home on a country piece of property with our Floridian furniture and décor. No one recommends using seashells in your decorating scheme when the cows are looking in your windows. There was nothing in the budget to replace anything at the time, and we just had to make do.

The people of Israel found themselves in difficult circumstances. The prophets told the people what to expect. God promised them that as they turned to Him and sought His help, He would hear their cry. Have you been there? Have you tried to make that coastal décor work in a country farmhouse only to be frustrated? Don't throw in the towel, He is working a great work in us to be of greater use to Him for our good and His glory.

---

design tip

If you are concerned about having too many different finishes in a room, an easy way to tie it all together is to add one accent color in various spots: pillow, lampshade, accent table, etc. The color connection can tie together those other elements.

FARMHOUSE

Thank you, Father, for the gift of the Holy Spirit who intercedes for us when we don't have the words. When the trials come, I am comforted by this truth.

It's Ok to Ask for Help

In the same way, the Spirit helps us in our weakness.

ROMANS 8:26

Are you one of those people who have a hard time asking for help? I am! I'd rather try to teach myself what I don't know to avoid it. Often, I realize after a significant amount of time that I should have just asked someone for help who knew what they were doing. In a fraction of time, a professional can finish the job. A decorator or interior designer can help to pull all the details together and has access to resources that we don't even realize we need.

While we are taught to go to the Lord in prayer, sometimes we don't know how to approach a problem or situation. When I don't know what to say, when the words won't come, and only tears fill the space, the Holy Spirit intercedes for me. He knows my heart AND the mind of God and prays accordingly. I am so encouraged by that knowledge. He ever cares and intercedes for me and for you!

design tip

An interior designer will tell you what you need to hear when it comes to your décor.
If you cannot afford the expertise, you need to ask a friend with good fashion sense and the ability to tell you straight what is working and isn't.

*Thank you today, Lord,
for the reminder to set aside the
weight of sin. So that I will run
the race you have for me with
endurance seeking to magnify
you in all I do.*

I Wasn't Ready for the Ironman

Forgetting what is behind and straining toward what is ahead,
I press on toward the goal to win the prize of God's heavenly calling in Christ Jesus.
Philippians 3:13-14

Designers disagree sometimes about emerging trends, what will stay and what will go. Furniture and accessory markets open for business twice a year. It can be hard to remember that these shows are displaying future goods—the things consumers will be excited about one or two years from now. That's why it's always wise to stay mindful of the basics. A classic neutral sofa can be dressed up or down and used for many years while still adding in trends in smaller ways.

Our Christian lives can be weighed down by our past sin. Remaining focused on our past, after salvation, will hinder the way we live for Christ today. Instead we run our race by faith bringing glory to Christ as a new creation.

design tip

I love to decorate a space with light shades of furniture with classic, clean lines and add in bold accents that I can change out throughout the year according to the season. I use this system to bring in pops of color I'm loving at the time through things like pillows, throw blankets, vases, greenery, and flowers.
—Jenny Caspers, www.acleanprismlife.com, IG @acleanprismlife

Lord, as I learn and apply the principles of walking with you, I pray that I will be continually and actively growing, never being satisfied to stay where I am today.

A Firm Foundation

Therefore leaving the elementary teaching about the Christ, let us press on to maturity,
not laying again a foundation of repentance from dead works and of faith toward God.

<small>HEBREWS 6:1</small>

I can't overstate the importance of a good night's sleep. A good foundation is an important factor when considering a mattress. Unless you have a platform bed, which has its own foundation built in, a foundation under a mattress provides a solid support to enjoy the place you spend a good chunk of your life. Foundations are important, but they are not the place you should remain. No one wants to sleep on a foundation—there's no give, and it's hard and uncomfortable.

We are to be growing in our Christian walk, not continually laying a foundation. Becoming preoccupied or worse even comfortable with only understanding the basics is detrimental to your growth. In reality, the growing Christian should be uncomfortable if they are not growing in the grace and knowledge of their Lord.

design tip

The growth of mattresses in a box in recent years has helped address the problem of replacing our beds in the recommended seven to ten years. Previously the expense and removal and setup process have been prohibitive, but now the convenience and lowered cost factor has changed the entire industry.

I praise you, Lord, for the patience you show me when I get impatient with your timing. You are an amazing God and I thank you that you are beyond the confines of time.

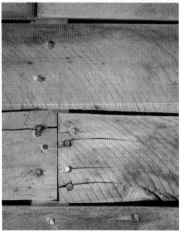

A Thousand Years

With the Lord a day is like thousand years and a thousand years are like a day.

II Peter 3:8

Building the temple and palace took Solomon approximately twenty years. Twenty years! We think design projects take a long time, but at least we aren't dealing with two decades! You can tell that a great deal of thought and preparation, time and energy, and money and resources were used in these builds just as we do for our own homes. Nothing was too good for the temple and based on Scripture it was Solomon's great pleasure to build something monumental for the Lord.

Sometimes I feel like it's taking forever when I am praying about something. Whatever our request we may feel that He is slow to act, slow to hear us, or slow to fix it. Our impatience comes from our limited view, and if we only could see through God's eyes we might catch an understanding that as the Author of Time he is not slow to fulfill His promise but is patient with me. Praise Him for his patience! He is indeed a great God.

— *design tip* —

Patience in the design process
is difficult for everyone.
If you order a custom piece,
be prepared to wait and be
patient. In the end, you will
be happy you did.

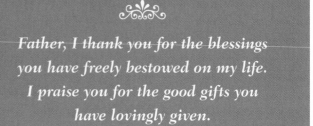

*Father, I thank you for the blessings
you have freely bestowed on my life.
I praise you for the good gifts you
have lovingly given.*

Nifty Gifty

So if you who are evil know how to give good gifts to your children,
how much more will your Father in heaven give good things to those who ask Him!

MATTHEW 7:11

Part of the fun of decorating is not only the shopping, but also the joy it brings to family and friends. Working with designers for many years, I've watched their joy as a client's eyes flash bright with delight after a project is completed and a vision has come to life. The same is true in our own homes when we find just the right thing that will appeal to the ones we love.

I love to find just the right gift for each member of my family. Many times, it's just something that I see in a store or magazine and I think immediately of that person. Do you do this too?

In a much bigger way, how much the Father loves to give us the gifts from his own plenteous supply. How it must delight Him to give us the things we desire and petition Him for. Why is it that we forget or neglect to ask? Do we just not believe the words to be true?

—— *design tip* ——

Purchasing home décor pieces as gifts can be tricky, but if you know someone's style and you make a great find, it can be a wonderful gift.

*Lord, remind me when I get too busy,
to step back and savor the everyday
moments with others. Help me make
discipleship a priority in my life.*

Sit Up Straight

And they devoted themselves to the apostles' teaching and the fellowship,
to the breaking of bread and the prayers.

Acts 2:42

A straight-backed, uncomfortable dining chair will prevent lingering around the dining table. If you desire to have family and friends eat and fellowship together, you need to provide a comfortable chair for the various body types who may sit there.

Those who walked and talked with Jesus also ate and drank with Him. They learned from Him in those intimate moments of breaking bread together. Our homes should operate the same way. For some reason, there are topics you can discuss at a dinner table that don't feel as awkward or difficult as they are at another time. A relaxed time that is unhurried and unrushed can provide our families, our friends, neighbors and strangers a perspective on what the Christian life should look like in all our communities. How can we demonstrate this today?

design tip

Sit in your dining chairs before you buy them if you can. If you are an average build, your feet should comfortably be able to touch the floor without banging your knees on the table as you slide in. If the chair feels narrow to you, it will likely feel narrow to someone who is larger than you and will be uncomfortable.

As I study your word, make me more like you. Help me be a diligent student of your word so that I learn to discern your words correctly.

Dig Deep

Study to shew thyself approved unto God,
a workman that needeth not to be ashamed, rightly dividing the word of truth.

II TIMOTHY 2:15

Great craftsmanship always stands the test of time. From William and Mary, Queen Anne, or Chippendale designs to the Eames, certain designs remain iconic. They retain their place in history and have entire styles attributed to them because the craftsmanship was durable. They were students of their craft and learned the necessary skills to make designs that people still shop for to this day.

We are also to be workmen! We are commanded here to study and to rightly divide the word of truth. This requires time and effort. Students don't just listen once and move on. Lessons must be digested, and truths become a way of life. Being a student of the word of God will require sacrifice on our part and diligence to dig for understanding and not just take a light pass at a passage and move on, but to digest the truth and apply it deep in our hearts.

design tip

As you place furniture in a room, space may dictate where you place certain pieces of furniture. If furniture must go in front of a window, in a bedroom for instance, choose a headboard that will allow light to come in instead of a solid piece that blocks the light.

Thank you, Lord, for having the perfect pattern prepared for my life. Help me to continue to trust your design knowing you already know the beginning from the end.

FARM TO *table*

let's STAY HOME

Perfect Patterns

And this was the workmanship of the lampstand, hammered work of gold...
according to the pattern that the Lord had shown Moses, so he made the lampstand.

NUMBERS 8:4

*N*o matter the style you decide for your home, you want to be sure to have a layout, measurements, and guidelines set before you begin making purchases. If you go to the store and attempt to buy paint but have no idea how many square feet you are trying to cover, you will either buy too much or too little—either way a disaster. A plan saves not just your time but money as well.

I love to read that even the lampstands in the tabernacle had a very specific design. They were hammered, made of gold, and more according to the PATTERN THAT THE LORD had shown to Moses. What a beautiful thing that the Lord himself planned the details so closely and intimately with Moses that even the lampstand had a pattern. When I am tempted to doubt and despair that maybe I haven't been heard, I can trust the ultimate pattern maker has designed something incredibly special for my life. You can trust him too!

design tip

Repetition creates pattern. Texture and pattern combined create visual interest
in wallcoverings, tile, and carpet.

Lord, help our home communicate love
to others because of the overflow of your
love in our lives.

Overflowing with Love

And hope does not disappoint, because the love of God has been poured out
within our hearts through the Holy Spirit who was given to us.

ROMANS 5:5

A home that exudes love isn't because of décor choices or furniture selected, rather it's the people living inside of it. Certain styles though do tend to feel homier. I think that's why farmhouse, shiplap, and Joanna Gaines have been so successful. A home that invites others to sit and stay awhile is more than just that farmhouse friendly vibe. The individuals of the home make the difference.

The Holy Spirit takes all the difficulties of this present life and He works in us the character traits that we need. Traits like perseverance, character, and hope because the love of God is poured out into us and then overflows to those around us. If we are not overflowing in love to those closest to us, we can be assured that we aren't overflowing in love with our neighbors or strangers either. May we spread Christ's love out of the overflow of our hearts.

design tip

Farmhouse décor is not going anywhere soon. The style changes slightly from year to year, but I think as many adults grew up and left their rural roots, a longing for simpler days and times causes many of us to put these items in our homes.

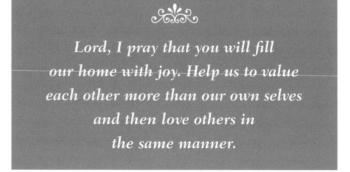

Lord, I pray that you will fill our home with joy. Help us to value each other more than our own selves and then love others in the same manner.

Joy Unspeakable

Then make my joy complete by being like-minded, having the same love, being one in spirit and of one mind.

PHILIPPIANS 2:2

I enjoy being around joyful people. Don't you? This passage prompted me recently to write these verses with dry-erase marker on the windows in our home. It had been a difficult season and I wanted our focus as a family to be on filling our home with joy and treating each other better than we treat ourselves.

Now you may not wish to write verses on your windows, no problem, but can I tell you there is no lack of opportunity to put up verses on your walls! Various styles exist to fit any décor and remind everyone what you desire to be present in your home. It may be just the thing you need one day to offer grace to someone else living in your space. A timeless reminder in front of our eyes to treat each other well and love as Christ loves us!

design tip

Whether a farmhouse style or classic and clean, verses appear in a variety of applications. Hanging a few verses in your room, can not only add beauty to your décor, but a vivid reminder of behavior we want reflected in our homes.

Create in me a clean heart, O God, and renew a right spirit again in me so that I can dwell in your presence and at your feet.

Clean It Up and Clear It Out

Let us draw near with a sincere heart in full assurance of faith,
having our hearts sprinkled clean from an evil conscience and our bodies washed with pure water.

HEBREWS 10:21-23

One of the greatest design fixes we must all employ from time to time: declutter the space and clean it up! The longer we inhabit a place the things we accumulate can take over. Sometimes when all the little accessories and pieces are lined up in a hallway or somewhere new, you get an idea for a new spot that piece would work. But when we get used to seeing something in the same place we don't even see it anymore.

I think sin is the same way in our hearts. When we are not paying attention, we get cluttered. The problem with sin is that it stifles our relationship with God, and we require a cleansing. Thank goodness He is faithful and promises to restore us when we confess and forsake. Let's be diligent to root out and weed out the clutter of sin from our hearts.

design tip

A clean space is refreshing and healthy. A sense of calm fills us when a deep clean has been done. This is a great time to assess if you need to purchase anything new or remove excess to keep some openness to your space.

Lord, I praise you for the calling you place on me. Help me to humbly and earnestly seek your face in each season and for each step.

Bloom Where You Are Planted

Now as to the love of the brethren...for indeed you do practice it...make it your ambition to lead a quiet life and attend to your own business and work with your hands.

I Thessalonians 4:9-12

Sometimes in home design we put far more emphasis on form rather than function. It's easy to do—we love beautiful things. But function needs to be a prime consideration in the purchasing we do for our home. Each piece should fit purposefully into the overall needs of the home.

We often complicate our purpose adding stress and anxiety to our lives. We are reminded to beyond loving others, lead a quiet life, attend to our own business, and work with our hands. There are seasons in our life when God calls us out to do more public service, but there are also times when He doesn't. We are to work in the place He's put us: at home with the toddler or an aging parent, in the workplace with the difficult coworkers, or in the public eye of ministry or service. God uses us no matter the venue, when we faithfully apply His Word to our lives.

design tip

The best items not only function well but are also made well. Look for pieces that you need while keeping an eye on what you want. Many times, you can have both.

you
are
loved.

Thank you, Jesus,
for the gift of salvation
and the grace that
is greater than all my sin.
Thank you for taking my
burden of sin and
cleansing me.

begin
each day
with
gratitude.

Robes of White

Though your sins are like scarlet, they shall be as white as snow.

ISAIAH 1:18

At the very heart of the color spectrum you'll find all colors combined into one single color. The sum of all colors is white. Decorating with white is a very popular design choice today especially in farmhouse themes and of course with shiplap! Variations of white with whitewash and shades of ivory and eggshell create a calm and relaxing environment. If you have a small space to work in there's nothing like white to create the illusion of more space. When our kids were young, we hesitated to use white, but many households today employ this color choice without issue. You have my admiration by the way—you go, girl!

Don't miss the rich meaning for the Christian and the color white. Christ redeemed us from the debt of sin that has weighed us down and has cleansed us as white as snow. What joy that brings me. He made a way of salvation for me and for you and this fills me with such joy. And honestly, living a life full of joy changes everything!

design tip

When you are working with color, you can mix metallics like brass with dark shades of black or navy, or chrome and stainless finishes with gray and white.

Lord, help me hear your voice to walk in your way, and to never forget that my time here is limited. I want to have done my best here and leave nothing undone when it's my time to go.

I Walk the Line

Pay careful attention, then, to how you walk, not as unwise but as wise,
redeeming the time, because the days are evil.

EPHESIANS 5:15-16

*L*ines create interesting aesthetics. Using the principle of line correctly in design and understanding the feelings different lines evoke can help employ other artistic elements like shape, form, and emphasis. While vertical and horizontal lines tend to be more structural in nature, curvy and angular lines create interest and movement.

Our Christian walk could be characterized by lines too. Mine hasn't always been straight. Can you relate? I've allowed sin and sorrow to knock me off course at times, but God has graciously brought me back. He reminds me that I need to pay attention to my walk, because I never know when my life will end. I don't know if I have another ten years or ten seconds to live the life that God has given me, but I want to live a life of abandon for Him. To accomplish this, I must be sure that my walk lines up with His Word.

--- *design tip* ---

Flooring that employs the use of a diagonal lines is far more interesting than most. If you want to bring attention to your wood floors, lay the planks in a different way and see what you think.

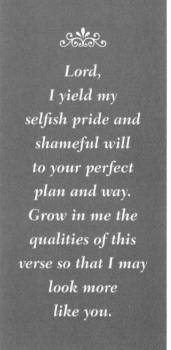

Lord,
I yield my
selfish pride and
shameful will
to your perfect
plan and way.
Grow in me the
qualities of this
verse so that I may
look more
like you.

Tooty Fruity

But the fruit of the Spirit is love, joy, peace, forbearance, kindness, goodness, faithfulness, gentleness and self-control. Against such things there is no law.

GALATIANS 5:22-23

A variety of natural elements are used indoors for decorating, not just plants and flowers but animals, vegetables, and fruits too. It's common to choose a color accent for the kitchen and combine with a fruit of the same color. Lemons, watermelon, apples, and oranges have all been used in creative ways to decorate.

Mentions of fruit in the Bible are many. The concept of being rooted and growing and bearing fruit is found in many spots. Being specific here when referencing the fruit of the Spirit, I believe it's important to remember that these characteristics that are to mark my Christian life are not something I can summon up to do in my own power. These are, rather, the work of the Holy Spirit in me as I yield my will, my rights, and my selfishness. If I desire that my life be marked by love, joy, and peace, then I must recognize my responsibility to allow the Holy Spirit to have His way in my heart.

design tip

Have fun using various natural elements in your decorating. Fruits, vegetables, animals, and more can find a place in your choices and in a wide variety of styles.

Acknowledgments

No one journeys alone. The path to publication intersects and merges with others along the way to provide us the greatest benefit of knowledge, experience and camaraderie.

I'm thankful for wisdom and insight from the team of Serious Writer, Inc. friends who are like family: Bethany Jett, Cody Morehead, and Michelle Medlock Adams, and including my agent Cyle Young of Hartline Literary and Junior Agent Bethany Morehead. I am incredibly grateful for Abingdon Press Acquisition Editor Karen Longino who saw the vision for this project and championed it forward through each meeting, believing in this book and including me in so much of the process.

An important part of my story includes my family. My parents, Glen and Jennifer Weeks have always believed that I could do anything I set my mind to. My husband, Rob Duerstock, listens to my great big ideas and never shoots them down. He has encouraged my pursuit of the dreams God has given me, and for that I will always be grateful. I'm thankful for our children, Kayla, Emma, and Connor, who have not only had to pick up the slack in the wake of my writing life but have also cheered me on with enthusiasm.

Lastly, because it is of the greatest importance, I am thankful for the Lord's intervention in my life bringing me to salvation, and the ongoing process of sanctification which brings me to this stage in order to write my heart on the page. I am humbled that He would use me in this way.

Contributors to
Design Tips and Photography

- Interior Photographer, **Justin Fox Burks Photography**, Memphis, TN
  www.justinfoxburks.com / Insta: @justinfoxburks

- **Julie Lancia & Jodie Kammerer** www.thedesigntwins.com /
  Insta: @julie.thedesigntwins and @jodie.thedesigntwins

- **Jenny Caspers** www.acleanprismlife.com / Insta: @acleanprismlife

- **Amy Stuckey** Insta: @the_refinedfarmhouse

- **Jennifer Ingram** www.gracious-spaces.net / Insta: @graciousspaces

- **Kelly Radcliff** www.thetatteredpew.com / Insta: @thetatteredpew

- **Caroline Bivens** www.carolinebivensdesigns.com / Insta: @c.b._designs

- **Sarah Symonds** www.graceinmyspace.com / Insta: @graceinmyspace

- **Jenny Zacharewicz** Insta: @bigfamilylittlefarmhouse

*A very special thank you to Stylecraft Home Collection, Greg and Meredith Drumwright,
and Rhodes and Kellie Thompson for allowing us to photograph your spaces and furnishings!*

About the Author

Victoria Duerstock is a writer, blogger, teacher, and speaker. With a mission to help women seek God's purpose in their lives and with more than twenty years' experience in the furniture and home-design industry, she uses her creativity to inspire hope in readers and ignite bigger dreams. She writes for the blogs Encouraging Women Today, Everything's Gravy, and Creative Corner, and has contributed to multiple devotionals.

Victoria enjoys an active speaking ministry to women and a teaching schedule where she shares essential elements to building an author platform through social media. Read more at VictoriaDuerstock.com.